What Others Are Saying...

"This fast-moving book challenges you to go beyond anything you have ever accomplished—and then it shows you how, in a practical, step-by-step process that you can implement immediately."

Brian Tracy, Speaker, Author of *Maximum Achievement* and *The Absolutely Unbreakable Laws of Business Success*

"A book that applies to anybody on the planet! Thought-provoking. Clever philosophy. Examples galore. Need another plus? It's delightfully entertaining."

Dianna Booher, Author of *E-Writing, Communicate with Confidence!* and *Well Connected*

"*Upgrade!* is a fabulous 'how to' book that works as a road map for continuous improvement for individuals and businesses. It will help you turn good to great, and great to incredible!"

Dr. Tony Alessandra, Professional Speaker, Author of *Charisma*

"This is not just a book to read but a book to do. It's packed with potential how to strategies to help anyone looking to improve the quality of their life. Super-fantastic job!"

Keith Harrell, Life Coach/Professional Speaker & Author, *Attitude Is Everything: Ten Life-Changing Steps To Turning Attitude Into Action*

"With *Upgrade!* Mark Sanborn has transformed a buzz word into the challenge of change/growth/transformation, not just for more success in life but for the privilege of being truly significant!"

Naomi Rhode, Past President National Speakers Association, Co Founder SmartHealth

"Mark Sanborn has the uncanny ability to make discontent a positive attribute! We are all discontent in some area of our life; Mark shows us a powerful, step-by-step process for turning the discontent into successful achievement."

Chuck Reaves, Author, *The Theory of 21* and *Your Vision, Your LIFE!*

"Getting tired of the old 1.0 version of you? Then Upgrade! and live the life that is waiting for you."

Jim Cathcart, Author, *The Acorn Principle: Know Yourself—Grow Yourself*

"Mark, you are both inspirational and instructive in *UPGRADE!* Your's is such a positive and unique way of looking at the possibilities. I will recommend *UPGRADE!* to all my clients."

Ty Boyd, CEO, Ty Boyd Executive Learning Systems

"*Upgrade!* is one of the few books you will read that will actually make a difference. It will challenge your thinking...it will confront your perspectives...it will inspire and motivate you to make the changes that are required in today's turbulent times."

Scott McKain, Vice Chairman, Durham Capital Corporation

"The time-tested principles Mark teaches in *Upgrade* can make even the seemingly impossible achievable."

Art Berg, Author, *The Impossible Just Takes a Little Longer* and World Record Athlete

"Sanborn is right: establishing and accepting the why is essential to an implementation of the how. Boost yourself in the true new millennium right: Upgrade!"

Jim Tunney, Retired NFL Ref, Speaker, Author, *Impartial Judgement*

"Mark Sanborn's *Upgrade!* is a powerful work. Some books have good ideas and some books help you see the big picture of a better life. This book does both and I recommend it unreservedly!"

Don Hutson, C.E.O, U.S. Learning, Author, *The Sale* and *The Contented Achiever*

"What a book! Mark Sanborn not only inspires us with his writing, he tells us how to reach the higher heights. And he knows how. This is a book you want to read, and then tell others to read."

Bert Decker, Founder, Bold Assurance Ministries and Author, *Speaking With Bold Assurance*

"If you are ready to find out just how good you can get, read *Upgrade!* It is packed with easy-to-implement, proven ideas that will launch you even higher."

Mary LoVerde, Author, *Stop Screaming at the Microwave* and *I Used to Have a Handle On Life but it Broke*

"*Upgrade!* is a non-stop read—it is powerful! A must-read for anyone looking to upgrade every aspect of their life. Your concept easily put personal power within reach of anyone. I highly recommend it."

Drew Miller, Publisher *Board Report*

UPGRADE!

Proven Strategies for Dramatically Increasing Personal and Professional Success

Mark Sanborn

Sanborn & Associates Publishing
Highlands Ranch, Colorado

UPGRADE!
Proven Strategies for Dramatically
Increasing Personal and Professional Success

Published by:
Sanborn and Associates, Inc.
818 E. Summer Drive
Highlands Ranch, Colorado 80126

Printed in the United States of America
Cover design and layout by Ad Graphics, Inc., Tulsa, Oklahoma

Library of Congress # 2001117383

ISBN: 0-9710926-0-5

Dedication

To Him
who makes all things possible
and to
Darla, Hunter and Jack
my greatest treasures.

Table of Contents

Acknowledgments

I am grateful for and wish to thank the many friends who provided feedback on virtually every aspect of this book. They include Jimmy Calano, Drew Miller, Eric Chester, Mary LoVerde, Scott Friedman, Dan Baldwin and my colleagues in Speakers Roundtable.

Special thanks to my incredible wife Darla for her editing, insightful suggestions and encouragement.

Introduction

Upgrade: an improvement, as of quality.

– Webster's Business Dictionary

Upgrading: a process of perpetual improvement in any area of business or life.

– Mark Sanborn

How Good Can You Be?

Some ideas are so powerful that they leave you forever changed. As an avid downhill skier, the 1988 Winter Olympic games had me glued to my television set. I was particularly interested in the performance of a 25 year-old skier named Pirmin Zurbriggen, Switzerland's brilliant all-around champion. This serene and religious young man was a fierce competitor who said, "I like pressure. I like to fight. I like to be at the best level of my talents."

I was particularly fascinated by his performance during the second day of the "Two-Day Combined" event. Zurbriggen had earned the first place position the previous day by .48 of a second, but only tied for sixth place during the first run of the second day. Overall, he was still secure in first place and even a safe, unspectacular last run would assure him victory and a gold medal.

Imagine yourself in the starter's gate, a shoe-in for "Olympic gold" and the recognition, money and opportunity that go with it. All you need to win is to finish standing up.

How would you have skied the race?

Zurbriggen exploded out of the starting gate and flew furiously down the hill. Suddenly, about two-thirds of the way down, one of his skis caught a pole and he went down—hard. Why had he crashed and shattered a sure bet for Olympic gold? Was he careless? Overconfident? Had he taken an unnecessary risk? I could only speculate, and no one else seemed to know. Two weeks later I was skiing at Copper Mountain in Colorado. I started a conversation with a ski instructor and learned that he was one of Zurbriggen's friends. They had even taught skiing together. I asked if he had any insight about his friend's Olympic performance. His answer changed my philosophy of business and life. He said, "In my opinion, he probably wasn't trying just to win a gold medal. He was, as always, trying to ski his best race." Most people are content to achieve their goals and objectives. Once they've accomplished the objective—gotten the job, married the spouse of his or her dreams, launched the company, or earned the money—they consider themselves through.

People like Pirmin Zurbriggen, the most successful of us, not only achieve their goals, but go on to set and achieve even higher goals. They operate beyond goals in the rarified atmosphere of the highest levels of human achievement. They are committed to the pursuit of their true potential, to answering the question, "how good can I be?"

The answer to this question is found through an exciting process that I call Upgrading. It's a way of thinking about business and life. Consider it software for your brain.

Upgrade to an Enhanced and Improved Version of Your Life

Upgrading is easy. It begins with a basic, yet powerful mindset and ends with an extraordinary life. The fare is paid with intelligent effort and the journey is the most fascinating and rewarding you will ever take. The opportunity to upgrade is an option open to anyone willing to take on the challenge and earn the reward. For example, Gillette launched the safety razor in 1903 and it was a successful product without much change in the intervening years.

In 1992 the company introduced a new razor with a flat handle specially designed for women users. It was called the Sensor. The Gillette Company continued to innovate and upgrade the product offering. In the late 1990's, following six years of research and a reported $750 million in research and development, Gillette launched its MACH 3 three-blade. To compete successfully, even basic products and services must be continuously upgraded.

You experience upgrading all the time, too. When you buy software for your home or business computer, you know there will be a new and improved version within a year or so. The 2.0 version will inevitably upgrade to a 2.1 and beyond. The opportunity for improvement is infinite.

Life is like that.

Options for the Journey

Even a quick survey of your business or life confirms that there are numerous opportunities for improvement. You can better anything: a product, ideas, services, lifestyle, health, relationships, contribution—the list is endless. And the means of improvement are limitless as well.

To illustrate the point, picture this. You want to get from New York to Los Angeles. How can you make the journey? If you have an automobile and a budget for food, fuel and lodging, you can hit the nearest Interstate highway or head out along the back roads. (For some the "scenic route" would be an upgrade over the interstate.) But would your present car make the trip without a breakdown? Suppose, you just don't want to put all that wear and tear on your personal car. Either way you can upgrade by renting.

You can upgrade further, budget permitting, by purchasing a new model equipped with air, power, automatic steering, stereo, Internet access and roadside assistance. Of course you can also leave the driving to somebody else and take the bus or hire a driver. Then again, while a bus is convenient, it's not the most comfortable mode of travel. So why don't you upgrade to flying on an airplane? There are many classes of travel and one option is upgrading to first class. Are there other upgrades possible?

Of course, unless you think there aren't. Our greatest liability is how we think. It is also our greatest asset. So, think again. (Now we're really going to fantasize upgrade possibilities.) Why not charter a private plane? You'll get options completely unavailable through regularly scheduled commercial flights. You could even go for broke (so to speak) and charter a 747 and take a couple hundred friends and relatives along for the flight of a lifetime. But why charter a plane when you can own one? I have friends and associates who are not content to let others fly them around and have purchased personal airplanes. They have their own pilots and some even their own licenses. (Even at that level of success, they are always talking about upgrading to a bigger, faster, sleeker aircraft.) Why not work extra hard, save up your pennies and buy your own airline. Now, that's what I call an ultimate upgrade. Talk about options! So what's the point?

The cross-country trip is just a metaphor for life. *Your* life. Your present situation is where you are at the moment. And at this moment you must answer two critical questions:

- Where do you want to be?
- How do you want to get there?

The answer to these questions will greatly affect the quality (and maybe even the length) of your journey through life. Wherever you're going, and however you're traveling at present, you have infinite opportunities to upgrade.

This book will show you how.

1

Why UPGRADE?

"I have offended God and mankind because my work didn't reach the quality it should have."

– Leonardo da Vinci

There's Nothing Negative About Positive Discontent

Most people believe in the importance of goals, but precious few see goals as pieces in a bigger puzzle. Rare indeed is the man or woman who realizes that no goal is a destination in itself; that no matter what they do, there are either different and better ways to do those things, or different things to do. They are engaged in finding their true capabilities; with performing and living as close to their potential as possible. These individuals have an insatiable desire to improve, enhance and enrich their products, services, businesses and lives. They aren't malcontents. They almost always appreciate their blessings as much or more than others. But the person interested in perpetual improvement, in upgrading, understands the concept of positive discontent.

What is "positive discontent"? The more common form of discontent occurs when we never enjoy what we've achieved because we're too busy trying to achieve more. We never pause to pay tribute to our accomplishments. As a result, we never experience joy in the pursuit or achievement of our goals. That represents a grave danger.

There is also danger in being content because we can allow our past successes to cause complacency in our lives. We live too long on the satisfaction of what we have accomplished rather than pursuing new endeavors or objectives. Positive discontent is the combination of gratitude and discontent. It doesn't discount or diminish what we've been able to accomplish but neither does it allow us to rest on our laurels. Positive discontent allows us to enjoy what we've achieved without the attendant danger of becoming complacent.

Alex Zanardi, the 1997 CART PPG Cup champion and previous Rookie of the Year, exemplifies positive discontent. He says, "My philosophy is to be happy and enjoy what you have in life each day, but never be happy enough not to try for more."

Most people believe in the importance of goals, but precious few see goals as pieces in a bigger puzzle.

How Good Can You Be?

You can tell me about your accomplishments, awards and recognition. But those things, though they are important, are a picture of the past, not an indicator of the future.

Marilyn Ferguson is often quoted as saying, "Your past is not your potential." For many these are words of encouragement. Just because you haven't gotten what you desired in the past doesn't mean you can't in the future.

Here's a different interpretation: no matter what or how much you've achieved in the past, you are capable of achieving significantly more in the future. You may have a net worth of several million dollars, have won the Iron Man triathalon, been awarded an Oscar, be wildly in love with your spouse and be your community's citizen of the year, but your past is still not your potential. No matter how much you achieved, earned, accomplished or won, you have the potential to do even better. You can better your best and upgrade every area of your life.

What This Book Will Do for You

This book is about perpetual improvement—upgrading. It will show you, in detail, how to be counted among the best personally and financially. It will explain how to create extraordinary results in whatever you attempt. And, importantly, it will teach you how to keep getting better when you're already among the very best.

If you're like me, you like to upgrade. We are always in pursuit of improvement, whether that involves hardware, software, business or personal life. Who wouldn't want to upgrade from coach to first-class, from a dead-end job to an exciting career and from empty relationships to fulfilling relationships? This book will show you just how to do it.

If you're a manager, why not upgrade to leadership? You can upgrade your customer service to create a loyal corp of repeat customers. Upgrade your communication skills and you'll go from impressing people to influencing them, from simply presenting to persuading, and from telling to selling. Upgrade an "okay" group of individuals to a cooperative force of dedicated people—a real team. Upgrade your job and you're on your way to a career. Upgrade your career and you'll be in the upper echelon of your profession.

What makes entrepreneurs different from other business people? You could say they've upgraded traditional business practices and processes to create new value in the marketplace. They are playing levels ahead of their competition. If self-employment is the upgrade you seek, this book will provide you with a map of how to achieve it.

Who wouldn't want to upgrade from coach to first-class, from a dead-end job to an exciting career and from empty relationships to fulfilling relationships?

The Inspiration of the Extraordinary

If you and I even came close to achieving our potential, we would astound ourselves. Occasionally we see examples of individuals and organizations who achieve such amazing success that it frustrates rather than inspires us. Instead of accepting that we, too, are capable of similar results, we discount those high achievements as anomalies. We should instead let them inspire us as role models.

Every field has its inspiration. As a writer, I am astonished by the works of Isaac Asimov. Known by most as a science fiction writer, he wrote more than 500 books on many different topics including mathematics and the natural sciences.

The *Left Behind* series has been a publishing phenomenon. Did you know that Jerry Jenkins, one of the co-authors, has written more than 120 books?

Those achievements could demoralize me as a writer. It would be easy to conclude that I could never write a fraction of the books of either author. Instead, I choose to be inspired. Why not learn about how they wrote so many books? Why not study their methods rather than just their results? Although I may never write as many books as they have, the point is that if I learn how they did it, I now have the potential to do it as well!

If you and I even came close to achieving our potential, we would astound ourselves.

Seven Reasons to Upgrade

Upgrading requires motivation. Without sufficient and compelling reasons to do something, all the techniques in the world are useless. It doesn't do any good to have the know-how or how-to without the how come. Here are seven excellent reasons—or motives—for committing yourself to a program of perpetual improvement.

1. Your survival requires it

I attended The Ohio State University during the reign of the late, great Woody Hayes, a truly inspirational leader. I heard him speak at a pep rally and I can still recall his words. "You're either getting better or you're getting worse. The status quo is a myth." In a competitive world, the most aggressive and successful around us, competitors and colleagues, continue to work on their craft. They know they will have to be better to get ahead. If those around us are continually improving and we choose to remain the same, in a relative sense we're actually losing ground!

To survive is better than to fail, but the best aspire to prevail. To prevail requires that you perpetually upgrade.

2. Your competition continuously upgrades

The lesson is the same in any field of endeavor: today's victory can easily be tomorrow's defeat. The winner of the marathon in the first modern Olympic games of 1896 had a winning time that, by 1990, was only about as good as the qualifying time for the Boston Marathon. And that year 9000 people qualified!

In the old days, you knew who your competition was. Today, you can't be so sure. Do you think the Postal Service figured on express delivery services like FedEx and Airborne? Do you think FedEx and Airborne predicted the invention of the fax? Do you think fax manufacturers knew that email would become an easy alternative to fax communication? And what new technology is about to be born that makes email look like yesterday's newspaper?

Your existing, identifiable competitors want your customers and will go to great lengths to steal them. Your colleague down the hall wants the same new job that became available and the guy or gal one floor down would like your job whether or not you're ready to move on. Your industry competes with challengers in other cultures with different tax bases, government subsidies and cheap labor. Whether your perspective is as an employer, employee or entrepreneur, it is clear that the world today is wildly competitive. Everyone wants to get ahead and they're investing in training, development and other resources to do it.

Every time your competitor improves, you've got to get better to meet the challenge. If you want to pull ahead, you've got to improve faster than they do.

Today's victory can easily be tomorrow's defeat.

---

3. Your customer expects it

The more you do for customers, the more they'll expect. The better you get, the higher their expectations. Your competitors get better too and in the process they raise the expectation level of your customers. You don't have a choice. When the customer wants more, you either get it for them or get left behind.

4. Your employer demands it

Whatever organization you work for today is faced with competitive pressures in the marketplace that result from cutthroat competition and voracious customer expectations. If you think you're worried, consider your boss. She has to meet the demands of customers, competition, upper management and probably shareholders too. How will she survive? By getting more out of every employee reporting to her. Your contribution to your company's bottom line must be continually increasing. It must always exceed what you're being paid or you are g-o-n-e in the next "right sizing."

5. Your friends and families want and expect the best for you, too

Nobody wants the significant people in their lives to be anything less than they are capable of being. Sure, we unconditionally love our family and friends regardless of their faults and failures, but if someone really loves you, they are going to want you to become the best you can be.

6. Your life is more exciting

A client once told me, "I didn't go to college to learn how to survive. I want to thrive!" If you were the kind of poor soul who doesn't mind spending 8-10 hours a day being mediocre, you wouldn't be reading this book. There are some people who seem capable of breezing through life accomplishing and enjoying little. Most of them are great at rationalizing. Deep down, I believe most people want to be significant, do significant work, enjoy the trip and leave some kind of legacy. But if you sense that being great is a bigger kick than being good, that average is boring and unacceptable, then you've got a fire within you that will resonate to the idea of infinite improvement.

"Once you fly, you will walk with your eyes skyward. For there you have been and there you will go again."

– Leonardo da Vinci

The better you get, the more you'll realize how much better you can be. How can that be? The beginner doesn't have any idea how much there is to know about a craft, profession, sport or hobby. The neophyte is blissfully ignorant. I believe God designed us that way so we wouldn't be too discouraged to try. Anyone who has achieved any level of mastery probably looks at the past with a sense of awe in how much they learned and how many seemingly impossible feats they were able to achieve. At the zenith of his popularity and recognition, Michelangelo said, "Still I am learning."

And I bet he was having fun, too.

The better you get, the more you'll realize how much better you can be.

---

7. Your success increases your responsibility

No man is an island. Successful people in any profession realize that they have a responsibility to be positive role models. One of Nascar's most successful drivers, Mark Martin, was asked why he was so careful about what he said to the media. Martin explained, "It's real important to give off a clean, positive image for our sport. That is our responsibility. I don't care what those basketball players say...'We didn't ask to be role models'...Well, you know what, it doesn't matter whether you asked for it or not, you are. You need to do the best you can to give the sport a clean, solid image not only for all the kids, but for the adults too."

Any society's role models shape that society's future. We need to be reminded what excellence looks like. We need to be stimulated by those who prove that any notion of limits, psychological, physiological and otherwise, are primarily imagined. Successful people who keep getting better remind us of the importance of the journey and demonstrate that ultimately, we don't yet know nor ever will what "the best" really is.

Successful people who keep getting better remind us of the importance of the journey and demonstrate that ultimately, we don't yet know nor ever will what "the best" really is.

The Very Best Reason to Keep Getting Better

There is an eighth reason to keep getting better, and it is the best reason of all—because you can! That's right. Upgrading—Infinite improvement—is possible, so why not do it? And maybe "because you can" is the only reason that really counts. Here's why:

I believe that common to us all is a creative imperative. We have hard-wired into our psyche the need to create, to fulfill a creative impulse. I personally believe this impulse was given to us by our Creator. As my friend Ian Percy says, education is the way in which we finish the creation that God began.

The gift of life is amazing. We all have the opportunity to create—to make of ourselves all that we can be, to develop qualities and characteristics that are noble, and to craft products, services and art that is edifying and worthwhile. Frankly, if that doesn't make some sense to you, you're probably reading this book by mistake. I can't imagine you're a "just get by" kind of person who read this far because you've got nothing else to do. I am writing to that person who says "I choose to better my best for reasons philosophical and practical, but a primary reason for my commitment is that I have the opportunity to better my best."

Education is the way in which we finish the creation that God began.

The UPGRADE Process

I have synthesized those traits and characteristics of those who practice the UPGRADE program which requires seven critical skills.

1. We need to UNDERSTAND

Learning has changed, and we need to understand the new rules. The best, those who strive to upgrade, aren't just "learned." The best have learned how to learn. They understand the principles and techniques that enable them to learn whatever is important for their improvement and advancement. They live the motto of the late Cavett Robert who said that school is never out for the professional.

Learning has changed, and we need to understand the new rules.

---

2. We need to PLUS

To plus means to add value. The best either create new value or they add value to everything they do. They compete successfully by offering better ideas, products and/or services than their competitors. They do more than talk about "value-added;" they deliver on it.

3. We need to GIVE

The best leave a legacy and live by the service ethic. They find their material rewards are matched or exceeded by the meaning they create in the process. They fulfill a passion for significance. They outlive themselves not by the results they've achieved, but by the way they've affected and touched others. Whether formal leaders, entrepreneurs or employees, they have a profound impact on others because of the example they set. They inspire through their own efforts. The best of the best institute formal efforts to replicate the principles of infinite improvement through hiring and training.

4. We need to RELATE

The best don't just use people as a means to an end; they build long-term success by building relationships. They understand that all results are created by and through interactions with others. As a result, they have become students of human behavior. They understand that strong relationships create loyalty and are the basis of partnerships and teamwork. The best network to develop distribution channels for their talents, and work well in partnerships with customers and teams of colleagues.

They are also highly influential. They don't just tell; they sell. The best know that everybody sells, and that he or she who sells best wins biggest. They know that their ideas are competing for attention in the marketplace of ideas. They enlist the support and involvement of others through their passionate ability to persuade.

5. We need to ADAPT

Most people view change the way most people view heaven: everybody wants to Go, but nobody wants to die to get there. Few initiate change for themselves or their organizations. But the best know the futility of resisting the inevitable and use change to their advantage. But they are not mastered by change. Instead, they are change masters. They make the most of changes that are necessary, and they pursue the changes that are profitable.

The best don't waste energy trying to put more time in their lives. They know this is an impossibility. Instead, they demonstrate that you can put more life in your time. They are stewards of their valuable resources.

The best don't waste energy trying to put more time in their lives. They demonstrate that you can put more life in your time.

---

6. We need to develop DISCIPLINE

The woman or man who becomes excellent and sustains that excellence throughout his or her life is first and foremost a master of self. She knows that nobody else can do for her what only she can do for herself. The motivated person takes responsibility for motivating himself.

Beyond taking responsibility, the best become failure proof. Of course they still make mistakes or miss their goals from time to time, but they don't allow setbacks to prevent them from trying again. They often use setbacks to leap ahead, learning from their mistakes and adjusting their efforts accordingly. They know you are only a failure when you quit trying, and that makes them paragons of perseverance.

7. We need to EXECUTE

The best constantly search out new ideas and techniques, but what sets them apart from others is their ability to implement more and better ideas quickly. The difference between excellence and mediocrity is often the difference between common knowledge and consistent application. The best act decisively and whittle away at the gap between what they know and what they do with the information. They don't just know, they do.

They also maximize resources. These are people who really have learned how to do "more with less." They have the same number of hours in each day as everyone else, but are able to produce far more than anyone else. They know how to replace money with imagination to extend the resources they already have or to create new ones.

In the Age of Mediocrity It Is Easy to Be Excellent

I once shared the platform with gold medalist and men's gymnastic team captain Peter Vidmar. He shared this paradigm-shattering insight: the gold medalists don't train that much longer than the other Olympic contenders. To achieve Olympic levels of performance requires, depending on the sport, six to seven hours of training each day. As Peter pointed out, no Olympian has the physical or mental resources to train an extra hour or two each day. The medalists, he says, are the ones who practice an extra 15 or 20 minutes. Or, as the saying goes in gymnastics, they are the last ones off the mat.

Consider your own life: your relationships, your financial situation, your career. Those who are doing better than you are aren't doubling or tripling your effort. The truly successful are doing a little bit more a little bit differently. That's what accounts for the gap between where you are and where you aspire to be. The reality is that most people aren't trying at all. If you want to improve, not just sporadically but perpetually, you need to know what improvement looks like, have a plan for achieving it and then commit the time to realize it.

The truly successful are doing a little bit more a little bit differently.

The Opportunity Is Infinite

According to some economists, Paul Romer has turned economics upside down. Romer is the leading proponent of New Growth Theory, a branch of economics that deals with the underlying causes of growth. Economics is the study of the allocation of resources. Traditional economic theory considers just two factors of production, capital and labor. Paul Romer's important contribution is that he added a third, technology.

Economists have typically assumed that all growth is dependent on capital and labor, or "scarce resources." Paul Romer proves it just ain't so. He wisely points out that we've always had the same amount of matter in the universe. It can be neither created nor destroyed; it only changes form. Romer explains that the only limit to growth—or improvement for that matter—is intellectual. We are able to do and create more with scarce resources because of ideas. The more and better ideas we develop, the greater utilization we get from those resources.

Romer says there are "two deep messages" of New Growth Theory. "One is that the emerging economy is based on ideas more than objects, and that you have to have entirely different institutional arrangements, pricing systems and so on to get an efficient allocation of ideas.

The second message is that there is enormous scope for discovering new ideas. When you're searching for the best set of choices in a number of possibilities that's that large, you'll never really find the best one. There will always be slightly better ones to be found."

Paul Zane Pilzer, adjunct professor at New York University and author of *God Wants You to be Rich*, echoes a similar message. Speaking of what he calls "economic alchemy," he says, "Traditional economic theories define economics as the study of scarce resources or wealth. In contrast, economic alchemy is the study of how to efficiently employ and distribute unlimited resources or wealth, primarily through the advancement and application of technology."

Technology refers not just to the hardware and software of computers and telecommunications, but to new methods and techniques. As long as we can come up with new and different ideas, we can continue to create new wealth. We aren't limited by the "stuff" of the world around us, but the "stuff" of the world inside us—our brains. The exciting news is that once we change this mind set, as both Romer and Pilzer prove from slightly different vantage points, the potential for improvement is—for all practical purposes—infinite!

That's what upgrading is all about. Let's look at how to do it.

As long as we can come up with new and different ideas, we can continue to create new wealth.

2

The UPGRADE! Process

> "The intangible quality that separates many successful people from talented people who fail is the sheer force of their wills. They have stronger passions, greater desires than average."
>
> – Alan Loy McGinnis

Jeff Bezos was 30 years old when he read a report projecting annual web growth at 2300 percent. He quit his job on Wall Street and drove cross-country with his wife and golden lab in an aging Chevy Blazer. By the time he had arrived in Seattle, he had a business plan drafted on his laptop computer. Five days later he moved into a rented house and started the business in his garage. Today that business is Amazon.com, the online retailer billing itself as the Earth's Biggest Bookstore. As the first dominant online bookseller, Amazon.com has 1.5 million customers. Fifty-eight percent of their customers are repeat buyers and they are generating $260 million in revenue.

Depending on your view of the world, you could say Bezos upgraded the bookselling business. Of course buying books online isn't for everyone. Some people still like going to bookstores, picking books up and thumbing through them before we buy. (That's an important point to consider: one person's upgrade is another's downgrade.) And the verdict is still out on Amazon.com's long-term payoff (big successes often require big risk).

Improvement is often subjective. Find enough people who like your upgraded version of an idea, business, service or product, and you will become a wildly successful and wealthy individual.

Becoming consistently better at everything you do, no matter what you do is a purposeful process. The best in every profession are those who not only learn from past experience but then integrate the lessons into the process they use in the pursuit of the extraordinary. I've identified key elements of the process of upgrading that you can begin using and benefiting from immediately.

1. Raise your expectations

Are you limited by your own expectations?

The greatest limitations you face in life aren't physical; they're psychological. That's because people rarely perform better than they believe they can. Beliefs about their abilities limit them as much or more than their actual abilities. Expectations either leverage or limit performance.

Before we can change the outer world, we must first upgrade our inner world. Bettering your best begins with this realization. Don't try for significant or dramatic improvements without first increasing your personal expectations about what is possible.

Challenge yourself by seriously considering the following questions about your own expectations:

How much money can I earn?

How much richer might my relationships be?

How much better could I do my job?

How much more effective can I be in utilizing my time?

Could I be healthier and happier than I am today?

Are you limited by your own expectations?

---

2. Identify the best that is already being done

People on the island of Bali have a saying, "We have no art—everything we do is art." To better your best, find out what the best are doing. Then do it better. Make everything you do your art.

Perpetual improvement can be evolutionary or revolutionary. An evolutionary improvement is to modify, upgrading and bettering what you're already doing or is already being done by someone else. A revolutionary improvement is doing better by doing something different.

You have two ways to improve: incrementally and radically. So why not use both?

To better your best, find out what the best are doing. Then do it better.

Three Questions

Three questions can direct your efforts at infinite improvement.

#1. "How would the best do this?"

Find an example of an individual or organization doing truly exceptional work. This will provide you a role model and standard. If you strive to be as good as the best, you at the very least better your personal best. But don't stop there.

#2. "How can I do it better?"

What kind of evolutionary improvement can you make on what the best are already doing?

#3. "How can I do it differently?"

Think beyond emulating what the best are doing and enhancing it. Think in terms of true innovation. Revolutionize something by doing it better by doing it differently.

Evolutionary and revolutionary improvement aren't that difficult! It isn't that those things are tried and found difficult—most people just don't try.

3. Always do your best...then upgrade it!

The next step is to ask "How can we improve every element of the product and the process that creates it?"

One of the world's most renowned restaurateurs was asked the secret of his restaurant's success. He said the secret is in doing everything as well as it can be done. He added that on his way to the top, he learned it doesn't matter if you're making French fries, as long as you make them the best French fries anyone has ever eaten.

Doing lots of little things a little better results in big improvement.

4. Quantify improvement

In Austin, Texas I asked a group of 200 insurance agency owners how many wanted to reach the next level of success in their business. Almost every hand went up. Then I asked for a show of hands, "How many of you know what the next level of success looks like?" Less than 5% were able to raise their hands.

If you ask most people what they're trying to accomplish, you'll get a list of what they worried about, trying to avoid, stressing over or concerned with, but you won't get a clear picture of what they really want. The problem is that you can't achieve what you're trying to avoid. Achievement must be directed towards the desirable and the positive. To better your best, you've got to know what that looks like. As a wise man once said, if you don't know where you're going, you'll probably end up someplace else.

5. Gather ideas

At this point, your limiting factor will probably be ideas on how to improve. That's why you need to gather ideas from others. Sources include books, audio tapes, video tapes, seminars, courses, consultants, coaches, colleagues, customers, vendors, friends and family. The ideas of others, when combined and synthesized with your own thinking, will provide you with many avenues for improvement.

6. Convert ideas into plans

The next step is to convert the ideas you find from conceptual into concrete. You must figure out how to make the abstract applicable.

I work in terms of "irreducible minimums." I ask my clients, "What are the three most important things your people should be doing to achieve the results you expect?" Beliefs become powerful when they are converted to behavior. If you've done a good job gathering ideas, you'll have far more ideas than you have time or energy to implement. It's important to prioritize. Start by identifying the irreducible minimums, or those three actions most important to improvement.

7. Identify barriers and limiting factors

The best way to deal with barriers and constraints is to begin by identifying them. Do an audit to determine what forces, barriers, obstacles or constraints are preventing the successful implementation of your ideas. Some of what you identify will be very specific to your situation. Other barriers are more general and common to many. They include:

No motivation
Complacency
Lack of commitment
Lack of knowledge or skill
Undeveloped skills
No plan
Poor use of time

Identify which of these barriers is holding you back.

8. Take time to practice

You need a training program. Every day presents opportunities to apply the concepts in this chapter and the balance of the book. Take time to practice. By that, I mean use single concepts or techniques on little ideas or projects to familiarize yourself with them and ingrain them as habits.

Remember that the drill of practice must precede the thrill of victory.

Remember that the drill of practice must precede the thrill of victory.

---

9. Play with it

Infinite improvement isn't neat and tidy. Experimenting is messy. Even the best ideas bomb. So through the process, remember: Have fun! Don't be afraid to test brazen ideas and implement wacky techniques. Develop prototypes, rather than finished products. Experiment with two or three customers before you spring a new service offering on your entire customer base.

And the ultimate take it out, play with it and have fun technique: do it or give it away for free before you charge. If the improvement process hasn't worked, who can complain about a product or service they got for free? And the people and organizations you give stuff to for free will almost certainly share feedback with you that will help you make your stuff work next time. In a story that is legendary, not only did Netscape initially give away Netscape Navigator, they paid hackers to find bugs and security loopholes in the software!

10. Get creative

One hundred CEO's were asked, "When it comes to explaining success in business, which is more important: creativity or intelligence?" Their answers: 59% creativity, 28% intelligence, 13% neither according to *Psychology Today* March/April '93. Interesting, isn't it, that most executives ranked creativity as more important than intelligence. Obviously, creativity is important.

You can be more creative. I guarantee that you can be more creative in the future than you've been in the past. If you feel you're already creative, then better your best!

Here are eight practical tips for how to do it:

Tip #1 Believe you can be more creative

Belief shapes behavior. If you don't believe you are creative, you won't even try. Our perceptions almost always precede our performance.

Many years ago I read a report about a creativity study commissioned by a large company. They evaluated their engineers and selected those who were considered most creative. Next, they did extensive interviewing to identify traits and characteristics. After cataloging hundreds of traits, likes, dislikes, beliefs and behaviors, they ran a statistical analysis model to identify those that could be linked to exceptional creativity. The most important finding of this extensive study: those engineers deemed most creative believed they were creative. Because they believed they were creative, they were always coming up with new ideas and experimenting with different things.

Belief shapes behavior. If you don't believe you are creative, you won't even try. Our perceptions almost always precede our performance.

Tip #2 Get instruction

Libraries and bookstores are full of books that focus exclusively on creativity and innovation. Find one or two or three that appeal to you. The best ones usually have lots of exercises. Creativity is a lot like learning to ride a bike: easy to understand conceptually, but eventually you've got to put your feet on the pedals and move.

Books aren't the only source of instruction. Free universities, colleges and public seminar companies offer courses of varying length. If you can't attend a live seminar, rent or buy a video or audio cassette training program. Learn from the experts. Let them point you in the right direction and give you practical ideas for increasing your creative quotient.

Tip #3 Spend more time in creative endeavors

Go to an art museum. Or a concert. Or the ballet. Or volunteer to sing in your church choir. Or join an improvisational group. Or make up a story and tell your kids. Indulge in anything that will get the creative juices flowing and expand your awareness of the infinite possibilities in the world around you.

Two types of information are important to creativity: logistical and nutrient.

Logistical information is directly related to the subject you want to learn. If you are an investor, you probably read a daily newspaper with an eye to events impacting your portfolio and investment strategy. You are searching for logistical information.

In reading a newspaper, you may run across an article that at the time appears to have little or nothing to do with a subject you are interested in, like investing. But upon later reflection, this apparently unrelated information provides context, connections or ideas that can be utilized. This is nutrient information.

Nutrient information is often underrated, but it is frequently where the best get ideas that give them an edge. My friend Dr. Michael LeBoeuf says to have better ideas, have more of them. In the same way, the more information you review, both logistical and nutrient, the greater the likelihood that you'll increase your output of useful ideas.

Getting instruction provides you with logistical information about how to be creative, but increasing your involvement in creative experiences will provide you the nutrient information you also need.

Tip #4 Engineer your environment

For many years I've been talking about how to create the right psychological environment for peak performance and innovation. I've come to believe that the physical environment is also very important, especially when it comes to boosting morale, creativity and productivity. A 1997 study of business decision-makers by the American Society of Interior Designers in Washington, D.C., found 90% think improvements in office design can boost productivity. To help stay competitive, the survey found, 68% said office design needs to be reviewed at least once every five years. Important factors to consider include lighting (experts suggest natural lighting), fresh air, open design and soundproofing.

Does your work environment inspire you? If not, where can you go—to a nearby park, a local coffee shop, or your study at home—to be more creative?

Tip #5 Practice

The most sure-fire way I know to get better at literally anything you want to improve in is to spend more time doing it. You've gotten the instruction, you've immersed yourself in the world of creative ideas, so now it's time to apply the information.

Here are several ways to get started:

- Pick a problem at work. See how bizarre a solution you can come up with. Forget practical. Make weird the goal.

- Redesign an ordinary object. A wheelbarrow. A coat hanger. A chair. Put your spin on it and give it your own unique name.

- Ask yourself puzzling questions. Here are some:

  How would you get people to buy things if it were illegal to sell them?

  How could you get people to a meeting on time if none of them had watches?

  How could you get your mail if you didn't have an address?

I interrupt these ideas to bring you a special warning: if you are a really practical, logical, left-hemisphere thinker, this stuff is making you mad. "This is stupid!" you exclaim. "How impractical!" you argue. That's the point. The practical, plain and ordinary aren't creative. Until you can break free of them, you won't create a better idea, product or service. For example, the parachute was invented over 100 years before the airplane in France in 1783. It was invented to save people who were forced to jump from burning buildings. Not the most practical idea for exiting buildings, but a superb idea later with the advent of the airplane.

- Use metaphors

  "Starting a business is like_______"

  "Reaching the next level of success is like________"

- Play "what if__________"

  "What if every employee in our organization worked out of his or her home... "

  "What if I had to raise $10,000 in 3 days......"

- Use conjecture to form hypotheses

  "More people don't visit my website because..."

  "The economy might crash because..."

  "People would save more money if..."

How badly do you want to be more creative? How much more creative do you want to be? Would you be willing to invest 30 minutes each day in the pursuit of being more creative? By doing that, you would catapult into the top 1% of creative people.

Tip #6 Stop looking for "the right answer"

The biggest enemy of creativity is conformity.

Our formal education teaches us to look for the right answer. If there is a multiple choice test, you can choose only one answer. If there are two blanks, you must fill in two words. Before we realized it, we learned there is only one right answer. Sanborn's Law of Creativity states "the faster you come up with an answer to a problem or challenge, the less likely it is the best answer."

The right answer usually prevents us from finding the best answer. Once we have a workable solution, why keep searching? The answer: because a better solution might lie just around the corner. Creativity is actually the pursuit of a better—if not the best—answer. It means identifying all of the right answers that we have to choose from and then picking the best one.

The faster you come up with an answer to a problem or challenge, the less likely it is the best answer."

Tip #7 Don't be bound by past experience

Try increasing your creativity by using "beginner thinking."

Peter Guber, Chairman of Mandalay Entertainment, tells about the logistical challenges faced in filming Gorillas in the mist. Beyond the challenges of filming at an altitude of 11,000 feet in the middle of the jungle in Rwanda—at the time on the verge of a revolution—the biggest problem was the screenplay required the gorillas to do what the writers had written. If they couldn't get the gorillas to "act," they'd have to resort to using dwarfs in gorilla suits on a soundstage.

In the middle of an emergency meeting called to resolve the problem, an intern suggested, "What if you let the gorillas write the story?" Everyone laughed and dismissed the inexperienced young woman, but later someone asked her what she meant. "What if you sent a really good cinematographer into the jungle with a ton of film to shoot the gorillas? Then you could write the story around what the gorillas did on film." That's exactly what they did, and they shot the film for half of the original budget. Guber points out that the young woman's inexperience enabled her to see opportunities.

Tip #8 Frequently stretch

Even if you like what you do for a living, it's important that each day we schedule in time for imagination stretches. You and I can be more creative. We can look at the world differently, through different eyes, if we believe that we can, and if we take time each day for imagination stretches.

11. Involve others

Discuss what you're doing with valued colleagues. When you reach a decision point, ask for advice or guidance. If you try something that works, but not as well as you would have liked, ask a colleague what they might have done instead.

The process of infinite improvement is most successful when undertaken with a team approach.

12. Perform post mortems

A post-mortem is an analysis "after the fact." Businesspeople use this technique successfully to understand what did and didn't work on a particular project, and how to do it better next time. After each improvement process, sit down and analyze—individually, and/or with your team—what did and didn't work, what you learned, and how the process could be bettered next time.

13. Refuse to lose

Don't accept failure as an option. Acknowledge that anything less than your intended goals and objectives means you need to invest more time, try different approaches or techniques, work a little harder or persevere a little longer. You choose to win! Those who better their best have the same approach to achieving their goals, realizing their dreams and living their aspirations. They don't play by some macho "nothing bothers me" mentality; what they do is quietly—or sometimes loudly—resign themselves to the fulfillment of their objective. Period.

Edward Deming died December 20, 1993. He was considered the father of the quality movement and one of the great thinkers about business management. He began his career in quality in 1947 in Japan, but it wasn't until 1980 that he really attracted the attention of American management.

Deming was consumed with teaching American business about quality. As he aged, his commitment and stamina for spreading his message never diminished. Towards the end of his life, when asked by a colleague how things were going, he said, "John, I'm desperate.

There's not enough time left." At age 93, he wasn't giving up. In the last year of his life, he led 30 four-day seminars despite phlebitis, prostrate cancer, and the loss of much of his hearing.

Deming created a body of knowledge that outlives him. He was trying to upgrade the pursuit and attainment of quality. He never gave up preaching the central message that "Quality matters, and it starts not on the factory floor but at the very top."

Even in the age of the microwave and fax, significant change and real accomplishment and infinite improvement—personal or organizational—aren't instantaneous. That's why the best persevere, continually upgrade and just plain refuse to lose.

Don't accept failure as an option.

3

Understand: The New Rules of Learning

"The only truly educated person is the one who has learned how to learn."

– Dr. Carl Rogers

1. How many birthdays does the average American male have?
2. Some months have 30 days and some have 31. How many months have 28 days?
3. Divide 30 by 1/2. Add 10. What is the answer?
4. A woman gives a beggar 50 cents. The woman is the beggar's sister but the beggar is not the woman's brother. Why?
5. Is it legal in the state of Colorado (where I live) for a man to marry his widow's sister. Yes or No. (You do not have to explain why to get full credit).

ANSWERS

1. 1. Mine is June 28th. If you answered "74", that is the correct answer to a different question. The average American male lives to be 74, but has only one birthday.
2. 12. If you answered "1" (as in February), that is the correct answer to the question "How many months have ONLY 28 days. But this question asks how many months have 28 days. The answer? All of them.
3. 70. This may surprise you, but 1/2 goes in to 30 sixty times. Add 10 and the answer is 70. If you divide 30 by 2 and add 10, the answer is 25. Again, right answer to the wrong question.
4. The beggar is her sister. Another answer, although really weak, is that the woman is a nun.
5. No. To have a widow means that the man is deceased which makes applying for a marriage license impossible. This question, however, is a point of practicality rather than law.

Most of What We Thought We Learned We Didn't

The quiz illustrates two important points. First, most of what we thought we learned we didn't really learn. Typically, we've heard the questions before and even been told the correct answers, but when they appear again, we still get them wrong. How can this be? Most learning is short-term. We remember the information long enough to pass the test, get through the course, graduate or obtain the certification. Then we promptly forget most of what we "learned."

One study of summa cum laude graduates from a top university administered the same final exams one month after graduation. All of them failed.

Saul Wurman says learning is remembering what's important. If you missed all five of these questions, it doesn't really matter. But are you able to identify the most important things to learn and retain for success in your business and life? We are deluged with information, it is critically important that we know and truly learn what's important.

Change the Questions and You Can Change Your Life

The second point is this: we used to think that leaders were people who knew the right answers. Now leaders are those who know the right questions. It doesn't do any good to have the right answers if you are answering the wrong questions.

As I've worked with managers in many different industries, I've observed them asking the question, "Who is our customer?" They believe answering that question will allow them to design a service strategy. Existing customers, however, may include unprofitable and therefore undesirable ones. A better question is, "Who do we want to be our customers?" Knowing the kind of customer that you want will enable you to design a service strategy that attracts the best customers.

"Answer your questions and question your answers."

– Eric Chester

Leaders practice a form of healthy skepticism. They know that useful solutions often have a short shelf-life. The important questions are continually changing: your customers, colleagues, employer, industry and even your government are asking different questions. The best continually get better by asking different and better questions than the rest.

We used to think that leaders were people who knew the right answers. Leaders are those who know the right questions ...

---

12 Life-Changing Questions

Here are some questions that, if thoughtfully considered, can change your life:

1. What are the 3-5 most important things you've learned in your life?
2. What would you do for a career if you had all the money you needed?
3. How would you spend your time if you learned you only had 3 months to live?
4. If you could change lives with anyone, past or present, who would that be?
5. In one sentence, what is your driving philosophy in life?
6. What is your purpose?
7. What do you live for?

8. What would you do if you knew you could not fail?
9. What is the greatest adventure you'd like to experience before you die?
10. What do you want to be remembered for after you leave this life?
11. What one thing would you most like to learn?
12. If you had to give away everything you own but were allowed to keep five things (other than clothes), what would you keep?

Learn How to Learn

"We now know that the source of wealth is something specifically human: knowledge."

– Peter Drucker

Disraeli said that all other things being equal, the person who succeeds will be the person with the best information. For the best, learning isn't an academic pursuit.

They learn, not just to know more, but to be more. Learning is a critical means to an important end. It is how they find the ideas that fuel infinite improvement. Here's how they do it:

1. The best make investigation and inquiry a way of life

Americans spend more money each year on beer than they do on books. "This explains," says Pastor Rick

Warren, "why our bellies are bigger than our brains." Theodore Levitt said, "The future belongs to those who see opportunities before they become obvious." The best know that the future belongs to those who can understand and prepare for it more thoroughly than others.

In *Leaders: Strategies for Taking Charge* authors Warren Bennis and Burt Nanus said that leaders are readers. Being a reader won't necessarily make you a leader, but the leaders they studied were committed to reading as a means of personal and professional enrichment. My friend Bill Byrne was on the cover of Fortune magazine as one of America's 1% wealthiest. A successful entrepreneur, Bill credits much of his success to his 15/15 program: He read 15 hours a week for 15 years. (Read Habits of Wealth by Bill Byrnes for more insights into how one of America's best continues to get better.)

The future belongs to those who see opportunities before they become obvious.

---

2. The best ask more and better questions of more and different people

The best use The Alexandria Principle. During the Hellenistic era (330 B.C. – First Century A.D.), Alexandria, Egypt was the intellectual center of the world, a flourishing arts and literature scene, and held the greatest library in the world. What contributed to the cultural richness of the city? No ship was allowed to enter the port without surrendering its books to be copied.

Emulate the ancient city of Alexandria. Query everyone who passes into your life hoping to identify new ideas, useful information and best practices that can add to your learning arsenal.

3. The best think for themselves

"It's not what we don't know that hurts, it's what we know that ain't so."

- Will Rogers

The best ask lots of questions, but don't necessarily accept what they learn at face value. They know the importance of thinking for themselves. Information received from any source is considered in terms of accuracy and implication. Don't accept things at face value. Consider what you learn from a standpoint of healthy skepticism.

Information, by itself, has little value. It can even be dangerous if the conclusions you draw from it are someone else's. As you learn, keep asking yourself "What are the implications for my career, my industry and my life?" Challenge what the source of the information is telling you to see if you reach the same conclusions.

4. The best choose critical thinking over the convenience of conjecture

The best seek the truth; they want to act on factual information rather than speculation and conjecture. Conjecture—unfounded or inaccurate information—can be dangerous. Acting on rumor or hearsay diminishes your capacity to live well, personally and professionally.

The best learners are eternal skeptics, not because they don't believe anyone or anything, but because they only want to believe what is true. Critical thinking requires continually asking three questions:

1. How do I know this is true?
2. Who says?
3. How does it affect me?

5. The best learn in future tense

Study for the future, not the past. Develop your learning agenda on what you will need to know to be successful. Anticipate what knowledge and skills will be important for the future and be honest in your assessment. You can learn for the future by identifying your limiting factors (or weaknesses) and your strongest assets (or strengths). But don't count on your current strengths to necessarily serve you as well in the future. And your current weaknesses? Don't worry about them if they won't be liabilities in the future.

Study for the future, not the past. Develop your learning agenda on what you will need to know to be successful.

In terms of future strengths (those things you'll need to be able to do to lead and succeed in the years ahead), start developing them now.

6. The best learn the most important stuff the fastest

"The future belongs not to those who learn best, but to those who learn fastest."

– Paul Zane Pilzer

Not that long ago, we defined an expert as somebody who knew the most about a given area. Their depth of knowledge and/or experience accounted for their expertise. The problem was, it took time to learn and experience enough to truly be considered an expert. Then there was a secondary problem: no sooner had you become an expert in an area than what you had learned either changed or became obsolete. Suddenly, you knew the most stuff about something that wasn't that useful or important.

Don't strive to know the most stuff about anything. But pay attention to what's most important, in the present and near future. Then learn the most important of the most important as quickly as you can.

When an area of knowledge becomes important, the expert will be able to (a) recognize the importance of that knowledge and (b) learn what's most important about that area (c) as fast as possible and (d) update when needed or (e) abandon when necessary. Practical expertise will be a continually shifting skill set.

Don't strive to know the most stuff about anything. But pay attention to what's most important, in the present and near future. Then learn the most important of the most important as quickly as you can.

7. The best design their own continuing education program

Almost all of our formal education was determined by someone else, but as adults, we control the flow of our learning. We decide what we learn and how much. That means we need to design our own curriculum. Few people have any formal learning agenda. Each year, I choose 3 areas of study. Typically, two areas will be related to my professional interests and the other to my personal interest. One year I chose to study the topics of wisdom and accelerated learning for my professional interests and guitar for my personal interest.

What is your learning agenda?

8. The best listen to their intuition

"In an age of information, only intuition can protect you from the most dangerous individual of all: the articulate incompetent."

– Robert Bernstein, former Chairman
Random House Publishing

A good rule of thumb for the age of misinformation, if something doesn't ring true intuitively, dig a little deeper. Here are some tips-offs: "They say...." Who are they? "It has been said..." By whom? And did they know what they were talking about?" Try to find a source and determine if the source if credible. Not everything merits further research, but if there are significant implications based on a piece of research or suggestion, do some checking. When in doubt, check it out. It isn't as convenient as conjecture, but you'll be much better educated if you do.

How to Find Fantastic Ideas

1. Commit to a leading edge reading program

I want to expand on how to maximize the benefits that reading can create for you. To better your best, read only the best. You can become an expert on any subject overnight if you read the best two books ever written on that subject. You will be able to dazzle clients with your knowledge of their business and/or industry by taking this legitimate shortcut. Rather than spending the years accumulating knowledge slowly through experience, rely on the knowledge of others to expedite your own learning process. The trick, of course, is to identify the best books written about a particular subject or business.

Take more time selecting to save wasted time reading. Spend much more time selecting books to read so you can read only the best and most stimulating writing. Why waste hours on a book that won't provide a fair return on your investment? Get referrals. As I meet knowledgeable people, I frequently ask them to share the titles of the best books they've ever read. I've cut years off my learning curve and uncovered gems of literature and self-improvement.

Spend much more time selecting books to read so you can read only the best and most stimulating writing.

2. Learn to multi-task

I am often asked how, for the past several years, I've been able to read an average of 100 books annually (I skim many more). The answer is simple: I multi-task. I take advantage of any spare time available to read. For example, the 30 minutes each day I spend on an exercise bicycle are spent reading and studying.

3. Listen and watch

I do not believe that even the best audio tape programs can replace reading for return on investment of time. However, as a diversion, ancillary learning mode or simply a way to get an intake of good ideas because you don't enjoy reading, audio cassette programs are values (especially when driving in your car. You convert dead time to learning time.)

If you have a visual learning style there is an abundance of educational video cassettes you can rent or purchase. Budget some time to learn through the use of instructional videos.

Learn to convert what was once "time to burn" into "time to learn."

4. Study the best

Dwight Stones is a legendary high-jumper. He competed in the 1972, '76, and '84 Olympics and finished third,

third and fourth respectively. While competing in Masters competition in the early 90's, he set five records, including the indoors high jump at 6 ft. 10.75 inches. What makes Dwight Stones so successful? I asked him that question. He responded, "I have no great leaping ability, and I'm not exceptionally fast or strong, but I have studied and learned the best technique. I know more about the sport of high jumping than almost anyone who has played the sport."

5. Retreat to advance

One of the little known techniques of the best is that they regularly schedule time for personal retreats. There are no hard, fast rules about how to do a retreat, but here are three simple guidelines. First, get away. Remove yourself from the daily routine. Secondly, don't spend time doing the things you normally you do: checking your email or answering machine, putting out fires and calling clients. If you do, it won't be a retreat anymore. (Give only one trusted colleague a number where they can reach you in case of emergency. Define "emergency" as a serious illness or death.) Thirdly—and this is the hard part—think. Reflect. Consider. Contemplate. And go deep. In these ruminations you will find not only direction but reasons for the actions that you so often take without thinking about them.

One of the little known techniques of the best is that they regularly schedule time for personal retreats.

---

6. Don't just surf the net—immerse yourself in it

"Give me a lever long enough, and a fulcrum strong enough, and single-handed I can change the world."

– Archimedes of Syracuse

Today, the lever of learning is technology. And the good news is that you don't have to be a "techie" to take advantage of technology anymore than you need to be a mechanic to drive a car. Anyone not computer literate today probably falls into one of two categories: unproductive or over-dependent. Those who are unproductive are relying on laboriously slow methods of searching for information (if they are searching at all). Those who are over-dependent are paying others, probably a secretary or assistant, to do work that they not only could do themselves, but would be better served by doing themselves. It is rare that a non-professional researcher can find the right kind or amount of information you need to maintain your learning.

The Internet and worldwide web offer an unprecedented opportunity to learn. Unlike the laborious and time-consuming task of library research in the past, anyone with a modem and web browser can access not just a library or database, but literally thousands of libraries and as many databases worldwide. Cyberspace is a playground for learners.

Unfortunately, many people only skim the surface of all the internet offers. That's why I suggest you immerse yourself in this medium that provides you unlimited access to ideas and people.

How much time do you waste wishing for or searching for information you know that somebody else already possesses? If you aren't able to utilize search engines to conduct a simple search, you are limiting yourself. Anyone can master the basics of searching the web in short order, and certainly for much less money than it takes to pay somebody else to do it. Will the process become simpler? Yes. Will it be to your advantage to wait until it does? Decidedly not. Leaders live and do business on the leading edge. They utilize new learning tools and technologies before they become pervasive. Your goal should be to be among the first 10% to benefit from a new technology. The leading edge includes those who wait—the other 90%—until they must adapt the technology to catch up. The best are always searching for a pre-emptive competitive strategy in how they learn and live.

A word of caution: while it is difficult if not impossible to be precise, some Internet experts believe that up to 65% of the information found online is inaccurate or completely bogus. Anyone can create a website. Combine the skill of surfing the web with critical analysis.)

The best are always searching for a pre-emptive competitive strategy in how they learn and live.

---

7. Join a mastermind or study group (or form one)

One of the wealthiest people I know is in his early 40's. After building an international business, he sold it and retired in his mid-thirties. He has enough money to provide him and his family an incredible lifestyle. Any work he chooses to do in the future will be for fun rather than as a necessity. And my friend is still a member of a study group. He meets regularly with a group of business people with similar interests. They choose cutting-edge books to read and discuss to increase their business acumen and quality of life. Most members of the group are in the top 1% of American's wealthiest. They are also among America's most voracious learners.

Napoleon Hill, in his classic book *Think and Grow Rich*, introduced the concept of a mastermind group. Here's how he explained the Master Mind principle: "When a group of individual brains are coordinated and function in harmony, the increased energy created through that alliance becomes available to every individual brain in the group."

Some ideas to guide you: 1) invite people who are willing to commit to the group for a period of time. You don't want members in your group who can't be counted on to show up. 2) Determine the purpose of the group. 3) Keep competitiveness and rivalry out of the group. The objective is to learn and grow, not compare yourself with others. 4) Spend a brief period each meeting sharing the good things that have happened to each member of the group since you last met. 5) Have a specific agenda for each meeting. While spontaneity can be a benefit, it is easy for a group of enthusiastic, like minded people to get distracted. 6) While social interaction is important, stay focused on the professional development you seek from the group. Friendship will develop or grow through involvement in this type of group, but don't let the social aspects overwhelm the intellectual growth you seek.

(For a free article on forming your own mastermind group, visit my website at www.marksanborn.com and click on "articles.")

8. Learn while you earn

Learning should be persistent, pervasive and fully integrated into your professional life. It can be argued that if you aren't learning in your job, it is time to move on. "When there's nothing you can learn where you are, you've got to move on, even if they give you promotions."

The objective of research and development is to increase value for a company through new or improved products. A company that isn't continually improving it's product offerings soon gets left behind. You've got to be continually increasing your value to existing and potential employers. That means you must be developing new skills and expertise through personal R&D, and that is perpetual learning.

All of these are sources for finding good ideas, including those that lie dormant within you as well as ideas in the outer world. But discovering good ideas isn't enough; before you benefit from them, you must capture them.

When there's nothing you can learn where you are, you've got to move on, even if they give you promotions.

How the Best Capture Ideas

We are bombarded by ideas every day. Whether listening to the news, attending a meeting at work or reading the paper, we are exposed to ideas that could be used to advantage. Why don't we benefit from more of these ideas? If you don't capture an idea, it goes out of your life as quickly as it came in. The best have a system of capturing useful ideas. In chapter six, you'll learn how the best implement and act on those ideas. But the first step in effective learning is the capture of ideas.

1. Create your own study

The best know that few things are more effective in improving your learning capacity than an area devoted to study and learning. One of my favorite rooms in our home is our study. It is lined with bookshelves jammed with books read and yet-to-be read, many highlighted with notes in the margins, audio and video cassette tapes, a large beautiful desk that I designed and had built, an oversized reading chair, excellent lighting, and a computer system. I have, over the years, put together my own personal R&D lab, and it is in this room that I spend some of my most productive study time.

2. Highlight everything you read

I have frequently been asked if I am a grad student because I can't read a book or magazine without a highlighter. I never want to loose track of the many good ideas embedded among so many pages and words. By highlighting the books and articles I read, I can quickly review and learn the key ideas each contain.

3. Don't "take notes," "make notes"

"I never know what I think about something until I read what I've written on it."

– William Faulkner

Note taking is copying key information. Note making is a commentary of your own ideas about the information: your interpretation, implications and how it can be applied. Good note-makers often use trigger words to summarize and remind them of key concepts. They use plenty of white space. Crowded , jumbled pages are uninviting for review and make it difficult to read. Many use a form of shorthand. It makes note-making at speeches and seminars easier, and is less-time consuming and taxing.

Note taking is copying key information. Note making is a commentary of your own ideas about the information: your interpretation, implications and how it can be applied.

---

4. If you can't write it down, record it

Some of my best ideas occur when I'm driving or exercising. That's why I invested in a digital recorder. This tiny recording device makes it easy to capture ideas. By simply speaking into a recorder, you can create file folders of ideas you can later transcribe or, in some cases, load directly into your computer.

5. Digitize to organize

I also use a Handspring Visor. This "personal digital assistant" allows me to maintain my address book, appointment calendar, "to do" list and idea pad in a device that can fit into a shirt or jacket pocket. I can "synchronize" it to the master calendar in my office by simply plugging my PDA into its cradle. Of course an age-old alternative, but still effective, is jotting down ideas on note cards.

6. Keep a journal

Many of the most successful and creative people I know keep a journal. While some may record the events of each day, the majority are jotting down their insights, reflections and information. More powerful than just keeping a journal, I've found, is periodically reviewing one's journal to reinforce the important things one has experienced and learned.

7. Make idea-hunting a weekly expedition

At the end of each week, search for the best idea you had in the past seven days. Record that idea in your journal, or your "Idea of the Week" log. By consistently recording those ideas, you will create a record of successful lessons that will put you in an elite minority of learners. Most go an entire lifetime without recording their best ideas. The best do it weekly.

Most go an entire lifetime without recording their best ideas. The best do it weekly.

---

8. Computerize the capture

Any of the above ideas, from journaling to a weekly idea log to keeping note cards, can be word processed for easy review and editing. Consider creating and keeping a lifelong learning disk.

How the Best Leverage Every Experience

Here are two powerful techniques to leverage our experiences for both enjoyment and instruction: study and reflection.

Study

The best leverage experiences by preceding them with study. Knowing more about what we experience helps us participate more fully in the events of our lives. Look at your calendar for the coming week. What activities deserve prior study? Is there an important meeting on Tuesday? Would it be a good idea to prepare by studying the issues to be discussed and formulating some salient contribution? Are you meeting with a new client on Thursday? Do you have a good background of information, not only about their business, but their personal interests, hobbies and passions?

We tend to think that study is academic, but the best study is practical. It focuses on adding to our knowledge, and therefore adding to the value of an experience.

REFLECTION

"Living artfully, therefore, might require something as simple as pausing. Some people are incapable of being arrested by things because they are always on the move. A common symptom of modern life is that there is no time for thought, or even for letting impressions of a day sink in."

- Thomas Moore

When Leonardo da Vinci was painting The Last Supper, he would work long hours but suddenly take a break. This annoyed the prior of Santa Maria delle Grazie who had contracted for his services. When da Vinci heard of the complaint, he responded by saying "the greatest geniuses sometimes accomplish more when they work less."

This is a surprising conclusion for someone like me. As I've aged, my life has become busier. There are more things I want to accomplish, greater opportunities and increased responsibilities. Being action-oriented and very productive at what I do, you can imagine my surprise when I found I could accomplish more by doing less. This past summer I made it a point to leave the office for one hour each afternoon, drive to the nearest Starbucks coffee shop, buy a refreshing beverage and sit in the sun to drink it. What I did for that hour was simply think. I did not take paperwork or a cell phone. I didn't use a laptop computer. The only indulgence was a notepad and pen. When a good idea came to me or I came up with an interesting plan, I jotted down some notes. Mostly, I just sat there and thought.

Here's what I've learned: The more I sit and think, the more I get done. Reflection is a powerful tool.

Conclusion

The best are life-long, persistent learners. An ongoing infusion of good ideas is the raw fuel for infinite upgrading. But learning takes time, and time is a scarce resource. Maximizing your scarce resources like your time and energy is the focus of the next chapter.

The best are life-long, persistent learners. An ongoing infusion of good ideas is the raw fuel for infinite upgrading.

4

Plus (+): Add Value to Everything

"In this economy, our ability to create wealth is not bound by physical limits, but by our ability to come up with new ideas—in other words, it's unlimited."

- Paul Romer

Ideas Are More Important Than Money

Money is the offspring of time and expertise. Time is fixed and constant—we all have the same amount each day. The best pull away from the pack in the area of ideas because expertise can be infinitely expanded. The best are able to mine more and better ideas from their expertise. That's what I call the art and science of "plus(+)ing." Those ideas spark an explosion of excellence, and often great fortune.

Most entrepreneurs use less than $5,000 to start their businesses according to the Bureau of the Census (1992

Characteristics of Business Owners). Only 24.8% spent more than $25,000 and 25.6% invested no money! Obviously good ideas and hard work are the biggest investments for most entrepreneurs.

Michael Dell founded Dell Computer in his college dorm room in 1984 for $1000. His idea? Sell personal computers by phone and configure them to meet the customer's specific needs. Today Dell is a high-flyer with revenues of $11 billion.

Phil Knight co-founded Nike. His ideas would reinvent athletic footwear and how it was marketed. Nike was founded in 1972 for $1,000. Today it earns $9.2 billion.

Become "Intellect Intensive"– Out-Think Your Competition

It matters little how much money or education you possess or the hardware or software you own. Your greatest resource is your brain. To better your best, become a creative analytical, a wonderful oxymoron if there ever was one. An analytical can dissect a problem, process, product or service into their tiniest component parts. A creative can then find ways to eliminate, add, reconfigure or synthesize those component parts to do each more (quantity), better (quality), less (quantity, quality or cost), faster (speed) or different (innovatively). Creative "analyticals" are masters of creating or adding value.

To better your best, become a creative analytical, a wonderful oxymoron if there ever was one.

Albert Schweitzer wrote, "The power of ideals is incalculable. We see no power in a drop of water. But let it get into a crack in the rock and be turned to ice, and it splits the rock; turned into steam, it drives the pistons of the most powerful engines. Something has happened to it which makes active and effective power that is latent in it."

"Folks who never do more than they get paid to do, never get paid for any more than they do."

– Elbert Hubbard

How to Create Value

Value is the output of applied creativity. The creative person can produce ideas, songs, products, paintings or a myriad of other items that are different, but not necessarily valued by others. When the creative output is appreciated by someone else who is willing to pay for the results, then you have value.

"I don't ever want to invent anything nobody wants to buy."

– Thomas Edison

The best go about creating value by considering 3 things:

- What they want,
- What their customer wants,
- And what their customer would want if they knew they could get it.

Value is the output of applied creativity. When the creative output is appreciated by someone else who is willing to pay for the results, then you have value.

What You Want

"It is so delusional to listen to the marketplace. It is fickle; it doesn't know what it wants. The best thing...is to find something that makes sense to yourself...and then try to explain to people what it is you have done. That works," says Randall Grahm of Bonny Doon Vineyard in Santa Cruz, Ca. He has been called "America's pre-eminent anarchist winemaker. " Wine and Spirits Magazine calls him a "California original" who has never been afraid to make mistakes and has never been embarrassed by them. Despite his eccentric originality, Grahm enjoys mainstream success. He produces about 50 wines and 34 are sold commercially. He has a James Beard Award for wine professional of the year.

What Your Customer Wants

In the mid-80's, Techsonic, a manufacturer of fishing depth finders, had nine product failures in a row and finally admitted they did not know what fisherman wanted. They did something radical: they asked them. They got suggestions from groups of anglers around the country about what an ideal depth finder would look like and do.

Techsonic designed and built a new depth finder called the Hummingbird. In one year they tripled revenues to more than $80 million and captured 40% market share. As a result of this unparalleled success, they developed a new slogan. At Techsonic, they had learned that "service and quality are what the customer say they are."

The beginning point of value creation is to find out what your customer wants, whether that customer is a client, an employer, a colleague or a spouse.

The beginning point of value creation is to find out what your customer wants, whether that customer is a client, an employer, a colleague or a spouse.

What Your Customer Would Want—if They Knew They Could Get It

Sony introduced the Walkman and the concept of a tiny personal stereo didn't come out of a focus group. It came out of the pursuit of utilizing miniature electronics. The chicken—in this case the Walkman—came before the egg—the customer's articulated need. Of course once the consumers learned of the Walkman, they had to have at least one.

The problem with product development, especially in technology, is that customers usually don't know what is possible. Ask them what they want, and they'll probably give you a variation on an existing product. Think beyond "articulated needs." Find out what your customer wants, and then aim higher.

Manage the Customer's Experience

I once dined in a fine resort in which the food and ambiance were very good, but the stand-out of my dining experience was my wait person. She was prompt, attentive, and pleasant. But what I remember most happened at the end of the meal. "Thank you for dining with us," she said as she shook my hand. Then she added, "And don't miss the comet, Halle Bopp, tonight—the sky is especially clear. Also at 7 p.m., you'll want to watch for the lunar eclipse."

No matter what business you're in, it is critical that you manage your customers' experience.

In those two closing gestures, a handshake and a suggestion to view the night sky, she added immensely to my enjoyment of the evening. In fact, the real treat of my dining experience had nothing to do with northern Italian cuisine! It was about courtesy and astronomy. She managed my dining experience so that it was particularly enjoyable, personal, and memorable.

No matter what business you're in, it is critical that you manage your customers' experience. It's those seemingly little touches that often have nothing to do with your specific business that will make your customers remember doing business with you as personal and enjoyable. While your competitors are managing product or service delivery, you can leapfrog them all by focusing on managing the customer's total experience.

Add Yourself to the Value Equation

Several years ago I spoke to a top salesperson who sold a particular product made by a large telecom vendor. As a matter of fact, he sold the same product as his competitors, but he was selling it at a 6-8% market premium. At the end of my presentation, I asked him, "how do you charge 6-8% more for the same product your competitors sell?" He said, "My customers don't pay 6-8% more for the product. They pay 6-8% more for me. I know the product as well or better than the people who make it. I am proactive rather than reactive. I know every client I call on better than my competitors do. You might say, the premium I charge is the value I create."

Reinvent Everything

In an age when everything can be reinvented, leaders must reinvent everything

I love Pittsburg's airport. There are lots of interesting shops, quick service food places and good restaurants. But there's also a health club. That's right. You can WORK OUT when you're at the Pittsburg airport. Michael Michno, a fitness buff from Ohio, got the idea for an airport healthclub after getting stuck at an airport for five hours. He and two partners proposed their plan to a dozen airports and Pittsburg was the first to sign up. Airport Fitness offers treadmills, stair climbers, stationary bikes, rowing machines, weights, workout clothes, shoes, t-shirts and shorts. They also have hot showers and a sauna.

In an age when everything can be reinvented, leaders must reinvent everything.

Do It More, Better, Faster, Less, Funner or Differently

There are at least six ways you can add value to any product, service, or job.

Do It More

More is an increase in quantity. Midwest Express has grown into a very successful airline from humble beginnings. One factor that makes them a favorite among customers is that all seats are first-class size. When you fly on Midwest Express you appreciate the added value of more leg room and comfort.

Another aspect of "more" is convenience. You can add value by making your product or service more convenient to use.

Do It Better

Better means increasing quality. Customers appreciate products and services that are superior in quality. When I first started flying on Midwest Express, what struck me was how they seemed to do everything other airlines did, only a little better. The company consistently received high marks from customers. All the seats on their airplanes are first-class size. You get a bigger, better seat when you buy a coach ticket. When you check in for your flight, you're offered the choice of two newspapers. The food is superior. I once had a meal that included lobster! On that same flight, they baked chocolate chip cookies in flight and brought them down the aisle in baskets for the passengers to select from.

Someone once asked me about their on-time record. I said I'd never thought about it—I was having too much fun reading the paper in a comfortable seat and eating chocolate chip cookies!

DO IT FASTER

The only thing your customer has less of than disposable income is disposable time. People hate to wait. Dominos Pizza was one of the first food businesses to make speed an issue. A hot tasty pizza in 30 minutes or less was their guarantee and Dominos carved out a huge slice of market share with this faster-than-our-competition strategy.

DO IT LESS

Can you add value by doing it less? You bet. Executive Book Summaries is an example. This service summarizes business books into 6-8 pages so that busy executives have less material to read. By charging less and delivering the same amount of an item or service than your customers could get elsewhere, you also create good value. Reducing overhead like labor expense by improving manufacturing processes or reducing material costs through smarter procurement or buying wholesale items for less through quantity purchases are all ways companies can give customers more for less. WalMart is an example of a retailer providing the same name-brand, high-quality products as their retail competitors, but for less money.

DO IT "FUNNER"

Is "funner" a word? Of course not. But it should be. Funner is an example of what I'm trying to get across: doing something the way everybody else does it is dull, drab and boring.

If funner was a word, I'd define it as an adverb that means "to add an element of fun." Pretty straightforward. And pretty powerful, too.

Here's an example:

Passengers on the 6:15 a.m. United flight from Denver to San Francisco are rarely at their perkiest. From experience, I know it can be a sleepy, uneventful flight. Of course, it depends on which flight attendant is on the plane's intercom. On one such flight, as we approached San Francisco, we were treated to some announcements from the unorthodox flight attendant who had been working the first-class cabin: "If you are having a hard time getting your ears to pop, I suggest you yawn widely. And if you are having a hard time yawning, ask me, and I'll tell you about my love life."

The usually sleepy passengers were waking up; there was laughter and giggling throughout the airplane. But there was more to come. After we touched down, the flight attendant was back on the intercom for final instructions. "Unless the person next to you has beaten me," he quipped, "let me be the first to welcome you to San Francisco. You'll notice that the airport buildings are in the distance. We don't land next to the terminal because it scares the heck out of the people inside. That's why we land way out here. That means we'll need to taxi, so please don't stand up until we are parked at the gate and the seat belt sign has been turned off.

He continued, "For those of you who are 1Ks, Premiers, and Frequent Fliers—there are too many of you on board to mention by name, but you know who you are—we thank you for choosing United for your extensive travels. And if you'll leave me a recent picture as you deplane, I'll be glad to mail it to your loved ones so that they'll remember what you look like. "My final hope is that when you leave the airplane, you'll do so with a big smile on your face. That way the people inside will wonder just what it is we do up here in the friendly skies."

Take a clue from this delightful flight attendant: Take some risks. Have some fun. And just maybe your customers will have fun, too.

Do It Differently

Stan Davis and Bill Davidson, in their book "2020 Vision," explain the importance of "doing it differently": "You can get 5, 10, 15 percent improvements in what you are doing by doing the same thing, only a bit better. But your competition will go for improvements in multiples. To attain 100, 300, 500 percent improvements, you can't do the same thing better. You have to do something fundamentally different and, in the process, your business will be fundamentally transformed."

The highest level of innovation and value creation occurs when somebody does something different. Doing it differently can range from costly to cheap. Ten years ago, the lettuce-in-a-bag industry didn't exist. Today, one in four Americans regularly buys pre-packaged, prewashed, pre-chopped lettuce. It's convenient, saves time and reduced wastage. Today, bagged lettuce is nearly a billion dollar industry and growing. For the past five years, packaged salads has been the single fastest growing grocery segment.

Dear reader, if you can reinvent lettuce, you can reinvent anything. The best strategy is to begin by adding creativity rather than capital. Intellect intensive people and organizations get more bang for their buck when it comes to value creation.

The best strategy is to begin by adding creativity rather than capital.

Value Is Where You Add It

We live in a society that values "new and improved." Simply claiming to have a better product, service or idea isn't enough. You've got to be able to demonstrate value by delivering it.

Often, the biggest improvements are built on common things. Bowling, for example. Bowling is hot again, in large part due to glow bowling, a.k.a. Cosmic Bowling, Xtreme Bowling and laser bowling. Here's how it works. The regular lights are turned off, black lights come on and everything glows: lanes, pins, gutters, balls and shoes (some centers have even installed furniture that glows).

Brunswick started the glow bowling phenomenon in the mid-90's but didn't stop reinventing there. Some of their centers now feature cameras that feed a 360 degree view of the bowling center to video projectors which then project the images of cosmic bowlers interspersed with music videos on giant screens suspended over the lanes. With fog machines, music and in some instances a laser light show, it isn't just bowling. It's an experience. Brunswick's efforts have paid off. Their research shows that 78% of Cosmic Bowlers were non-league bowlers and 84% are under the age of 34. Their reinvention of an old sport enables them to cater to a new market of bowlers.

That's the power of "plusing:" the ability to add value to everything you do. And now I'd like to add to your storehouse of valuable knowledge by asking you to move on to the next chapter.

5

Give: From Go-Getter to Go-Giver

"No man can become rich without himself enriching others."

– Andrew Carnegie

Here's one of the best kept secrets of contemporary life: you can't do something nice for someone without getting richly rewarded yourself. This principle applies to every area of our lives.

Several years ago I worked with Big O Tires based in Englewood, Colorado. Admittedly, it is easy to get people to spend more money on tires than is necessary and disreputable tire dealers continually take advantage of customers. Big O Tires had a commitment to building loyal customers by being honest and giving good value and great service. At the time, they had a corporate slogan that impressed me. They called this approach "doing unselfish things for selfish reasons." Big O knew that by treating their customers right they would be rewarded with loyalty and repeat business. They were acknowledging in different words the principle I just related.

You can't do something nice for someone without getting richly rewarded yourself.

The motive behind customer service is profit: give better service and you'll earn more. Customer service done well pays well. And there is nothing wrong with that. I call it the service ethic. The problem seems to me to be that people have the ability to take a good idea and corrupt it. For instance: have you ever tried to get change for a dollar bill in a mall? It wouldn't be unusual to get this response, "I'm sorry, but I can't give you change unless you buy something." Suddenly it seems like you only get service if you buy it. If you don't pay for it, you don't get a little needed assistance.

For most today, the message of customer service is "do it because it is profitable." The message of the service ethic is "do it because it is the right thing to do." I believe when you do the right thing you always profit from it. It may not be a monetary payoff, but the gratification, the satisfaction, the sense of having done something kind—all have their own kind of rewards. Not only do those acts of service benefit others, I would argue that they make you and I better people.

"Always do right. This will gratify some people and astonish the rest."

– Mark Twain

Our habits shape us. While it is true that good people tend to do good things, it is important to remember that doing good things can make us good. We can resist any impulse towards selfishness or self-absorption by doing those things that a good person would do. Successful people do the right things because they need to and can. We can triumph over petty feelings by choosing better actions—actions to help, serve, assist, donate and contribute—and those actions make us better people in the process.

James Dobson makes an interesting point on the theology of tithing. Biblically, believers are asked to give 10% of their earnings to the church. Dobson says that God doesn't command us to give because he needs the money—obviously God doesn't! God commands us to give because we need to learn how to give.

William James, the great early American psychologist, said, "The only truly happy people I know are those who have found a cause greater than themselves to live for." The best have purposes while the rest have only reasons. One of the great existential questions begged by the challenge of service is simply the question "Why?" Why give of myself or my time? What does this have to do with bettering my best?

I have often heard successful men and women say, "I want to put something back into the system since I've gotten so much out." This initially rings true. If a community, university or industry has presented opportunities that made individuals wildly successful, it would follow that those individuals might be compelled to contribute back into that system. But let me challenge your thinking. If you and I only put back as much as we took out, have we truly contributed? Is that not, instead, just barter? Isn't that simply a zero-sum game?

The best have purposes while the rest have only reasons.

Here is a radical idea for those who desire to better their best: the highest contribution occurs when you put more back into the system than you took out! Are there people who contribute more to a community or society than the community or society ever gave them? Those people better their best by moving beyond simple success to unselfish service.

The Need for a Philosophy

"When the Who's Who editors forced me to epitomize my life and work, I wrote to them and said, 'I have seen the meaning of my life in helping others to see in their lives a meaning.'"

- Viktor Frankl

The opportunity to be of service is abundant. One needs only to look at the world seriously for a moment to realize the incredible need that exists in a planet of plenty.

My own philosophy of service to others is based on these three beliefs:

1. The everyday experience of life for an individual or organization is one of pain; that is, pain is normative.
2. Everyday experience offers the opportunity for unlimited joy despite the pain.

3. I can serve whenever I help people understand the pain, deal with it, experience the joy or, the best option, do all three.

Admitting, Understanding & Responding to Pain

I first heard David Yoho, Sr. speak while I was still a student at The Ohio State University. A powerful speaker, Dave perplexed me when he said "Everybody hurts."

I thought that was a dismal view for a motivational speaker to hold. Life experience since has convinced me of that truth. For many, homelessness and hunger are a daily and real pain. But even those whose physical needs are met experience pains of differing kinds. No matter how successful we are, life is painful. Personal tragedy is a daily occurrence for many we encounter each day.

A quick survey of American businesses will prove the same is true about organizational pain: foundation-shaking changes, layoffs at every level, displacement, diminishing resources and uncertainty are "business as usual." Even those companies that are currently successful realize (or should) that the distance from super-star to dinosaur is a short distance indeed.

I recently watched as the CEO of a large corporation spoke to his distributors about the organization's problems and mistakes. His optimism for the future thinly veiled his anguish. Not all people or organizations that hurt admit it. Denial is common and dysfunction is a symptom of unresolved pain. Many, myself included, have tried to deal with the pain by ignoring it or anesthetizing it with activity. Both are costly and ineffective strategies.

For many reasons, we are unwilling to deal with the reality of pain. There seems to be a social stigma that says people/organizations that hurt aren't as good as those who don't. In reality, they are usually the healthiest if they can experience hurt and move through the pain instead of becoming mired in it. An outsider can help by making it okay to admit pain.

Beyond an unwillingness to admit pain, there is a problem understanding why we are in pain. Understanding becomes our first step in coping. You can be of value to people in helping them understand their challenges, giving them encouragement and helping them plot a course to address their pain.

We can also demonstrate the opportunity for joy despite the pain. If there must be an absence of pain for joy to exist, the condition of the average person and organization is hopeless. When an individual or organization becomes fixated on their pain, all other awareness diminishes. Sometimes all we need to do is increase the scope of their vision. We can also offer encouragement and strategies for experiencing joy.

Even when I work with clients enjoying high levels of success, there is always the recognition that difficulty could be just around the corner. Just as the rational organization can hope for joy despite pain, the rational organization should plan for potential downturn or failure in times of victory. If we want to be of service to individuals and organizations, we can help them use this eternal tension of pain/joy to their advantage.

The Bigger Picture

The best in every profession often rise to a level of leadership distinguished by their service to others. They become as well known for what they do for others as for what they've accomplished for themselves. Harriet Rubin said, "...the ultimate measure of your success is to realize that you don't have to be recognized for your work—because you're making a contribution."

"I want to use television not only to entertain but to help people lead better lives," says Oprah Winfrey, whom Forbes estimates has a personal fortune of $550 million. She has an incredible potential to do so with 20 million faithful viewers who watch her on 206 stations nationwide in some 132 countries. She has not only the power, but the time to be of service. But what about the common man or woman?

A member of the congregation at Willow Creek Community Church in Barrington Heights, Illinois, approached Pastor Bill Hybels. He was a mechanic, and wanted to contribute to the ministry of serving people. Weren't there people who needed reliable cars for transportation to work? To get their kids to school? And maybe these people couldn't afford costly repairs that were needed. The mechanic would contribute his time to fix the cars if the church would pay for the parts. The idea was approved, and before long the mechanic had enlisted others to assist him in "the cars ministry." A few months later, the same mechanic approached Hybels again. Weren't there wealthy people in the church who had cars they needed to get rid of? Maybe those rich people would donate the cars to the church for a tax write-off? The cars ministry would fix 'em up and provide them for people in need who couldn't afford reliable transportation.

Since that time, the cars ministry at Willow Creek has grown large and served many. A successful and extremely valuable ministry was born from the idea of one man who desired to use his skills as a mechanic to be of service.

Johnny Johnson, CEO of Richmond's Community Pride Stores gave a ride home to a shopper he'd seen standing in the rain outside one of his markets. The customer remarked that he'd buy more groceries if he always had a way to get home. Today, the grocery chain has a fleet of 14 vans hauling customers to his seven inner-city stores. The van service, by the way, increased his business 21% the first year.

He also gives a 5% discount to elderly shoppers, and has installed PCs equipped with financial aid packages in area high schools. He wants to put "the neighborhood back into the 'hood." Why?

"When it all boils down, everybody is selling the same canned goods. But what is important is what we do with that penny we hope to make off those canned goods. We're going to pick your grandmother up and bring her to the store every Tuesday. We're going to take you home when you don't have a ride. We spend between $33,000 and $40,000 every nine weeks in our High Achievement Program, which recognizes academic and attendance excellence in Richmond Public School students. That is how we align ourselves with customers. We call it institutional advertising and marketing. We invest back into the community, and people really appreciate that.

Johnson calls it institutional advertising and marketing. I call it doing the right thing. The best know that they can be of service whoever they are by using what they already know and do so well to be of greater service to others.

"Self is the only prison that can bind the soul."

– Henry Van Dyke

Self-absorption is a barrier to service. Upgrading is about being the best human being you can be. If that is the goal, the other roles in your life will improve proportionately. He or she who is preoccupied only with him- or herself doesn't notice the opportunity, much less the need to be of service to others.

Many years ago psychologists conducted an interesting study. They told students that the study was a test for verbal retention. In reality, that was not the goal. Half of the students in the test were read the parable of the good Samaritan from the Bible. The other half were read entirely different passages. In the hallway outside the testing room, an actor was lying on the floor and looking battered. Not many students stopped to help the man, and only slightly more stopped that had heard the parable of the good Samaritan. Some of the students who had heard the parable were told to "hurry along" to the other end of the hall. None of them stopped to help the man! Being in a hurry blinded them, and prevented them from being of service.

Self-absorption is a barrier to service. Upgrading is about being the best human being you can be. If that is the goal, the other roles in your life will improve proportionately.

Bettering your best isn't about making more money. Bettering your best is about becoming the best you can be and continuing to improve. The best you can be isn't as a businessperson, consultant, author, salesperson, husband, wife, mother or father—ultimately it is about being the best human being you can be. If that is the goal, the other roles in your life will improve proportionately.

"We can do no great things—only small things with great love."

- Mother Teresa

The Marks We Leave

As time goes on and we reflect
On the things we've said and done;
The places we've been, the people we've met
And we think of all the fun.

We realize the marks we leave in life
Aren't made of stone or steel
But rather of the lives we've touched
And how we make folks feel.

For people are far more valuable
Than achievements great and high,
Than cars or planes or space shuttles
Or buildings reaching to the sky.

You and I can leave our mark in life
By doing all we can
To serve and praise and uplift
The lives of children, women and men.

- Mark Sanborn, CSP, CPAE

6

Relate

"It doesn't make much difference how much other knowledge or experience an executive possesses; if he is unable to achieve results through people, he is worthless as an executive."

– J. Paul Getty

Answer yes or no to the following questions:

___ My drive to improve and succeed has not damaged my relationships.

___ I am not hindered in my success personally or professionally by problematic relationships.

___ The primary groups I participate in practice teamwork.

___ I partner successfully in my professional pursuits.

___ Others believe in what I do and offer support.

___ Compared with my competitors, I do a better job of understanding and serving my customers, colleagues and vendors.

___ I enjoy the quality of my relationships with others.

___ My communications are clear and kind; I am rarely misunderstood or resented for how I conveyed my message.

___ I can name 2-3 little things I did today to prove to others that I value them.

Unless you've answered a resounding yes to every one of those questions, you've got opportunities to upgrade your relationships. The road to success is often littered with many damaged or ruined relationships. High performers often have a tendency to be task or outcome-focused, and relationships can suffer as a result. It doesn't have to be that way.

Relationships Are Everything

We are social creatures. We don't live in a vacuum. I recall a college recruiter who told me he would throw up if another interviewee told him they wanted "to work with people." "That's the only way anybody works," he said.

The single greatest success skill we ever develop in life is the ability to build healthy relationships with other people.

It affects the quality and quantity of our friendships. It determines the success of our marriages and the rewards of our parenting.

It leverages our abilities to achieve results through partnering and teaming with others.

The best in any field keep getting better by creating new relationships or improving existing ones.

The single greatest success skill we ever develop in life is the ability to build healthy relationships with other people.

Healthy Relationships Are Never Exploitative

That does not imply that people are a means to an end. A manipulative individual uses people to achieve results or rewards. But that ploy is easily recognized. We recognize them as someone who has succumbed to the worst that a focus on results and rewards represents.

Power with people is about treating others with dignity and respect; about helping them meet their needs, not manipulating them to meet our own. True success is ethical success. Using others to achieve results or rewards is a hollow victory. That's a practice not of the best, but of the worst in our world.

How to Build Better Relationships

Relationship building can be tough. You can't do spreadsheet analysis on it. You can't number crunch "relationship quality." Relationship building is ephemeral and qualitative. Yet your ability to build better relationships is critical to your ability to better your best. Here are some simple things you can do to build more and better relationships with others:

1. Initiate contact

One day I slipped into the room to where I'd be speaking to watch the meeting. I sat in the back row. The guy next to me turned, "Hey, I'm Tim," he said warmly, extending his hand, "and this is my wife Tina."

"I'm Mark, the speaker guy," I joked. "Yea, I know. I read your bio in the program. Went to Ohio State, huh? I just moved to Charlotte from Cincinnati..." and with that, he was off, and we were talking like old friends. Before I got up to speak, he handed me his business card. "You're ever in Charlotte, give us a call and we'll grab a bite to eat or have a beer." Tim was a sterling example of the best. When it comes to establishing relationships, the best initiate.

The best know the importance of taking the lead. The best target those they want to get to know, and they aren't afraid to make contact. They mingle and network and they enjoy meeting new people.

2. Ask more and better questions

When the late poll Thomas "Tip" O'Neil was running for Cambridge City Council in 1934 and the day of the election arrived, he encountered a neighbor who said he was going to vote for him even though he hadn't ask her to. This surprised O'Neil. He said, "I've lived across the street from you for eighteen years. I shovel your walk in the winter and I mow your grass in the summer. I didn't think I needed to ask you for your vote," he said. "Tom, I want you to know something," the woman replied, "people like to be asked."

I've found that you can improve your success in life if you ask the right questions of the right people.

You can improve your success in life if you ask the right questions of the right people.

---

3. Search out the best in others

The best look for the best in others; the rest quickly identify the worst. It is easy to be critical. Nearly everyone we meet has imperfections and weaknesses. For some reason, it is easy to quickly detect them, but building relationships means building on strengths. We are drawn to those who recognize our abilities and potential rather than our deficits and pitfalls.

It is easy to spot the faults and deficits in others. There is no talent required for doing that. The best learn to uncover the best in others. Where most see problems, the best see possibilities. A manager sees an employee who clowns around too much; a leader sees someone whose sense of humor cheers her colleagues.

The best look for the good in others.

4. Treat others the way others want to be treated

"No matter how much you like vegetables yourself, never try to feed a cat a carrot."

– Alex McEachern

My friend Tony Alessandra calls it the Platinum Principle, a modern twist on The Golden Rule which says "do unto others as you would have them do unto you." Jesus spoke these profound words. The Platinum Rule is "do unto others as they would have you do unto them." The other man or woman may not share your preferences or enthusiasms. Why not find out what they like, and then provide it?

How do the best know how others want to be treated? That's the next key.

5. Make the effort and take the time to truly understand

In the mid-80's I was testing a new program for a public seminar company called "How To Motivate People." I discussed many principles and practices of motivating both self and others. I was suddenly moved to do some quick and dirty research. "How many of you," I asked the 300 people assembled, "have been asked by any employer at any point in your career, the question, 'What motivates you?'" Less than 15% raised their hands. The insight was dramatic. 85% of our efforts to motivate others are based on guesses and assumptions. We seldom do the hard but necessary work of finding out what motivates others.

The best take the time to truly understand the important people around them.

6. Partner

There are times when a team member has to take the lead in a project. Doing that requires the committed support of other team members. A team member won't take necessary risks and put themselves on the line to innovate and succeed unless they know they are supported. At the same time, leaders are called upon to support their teammates. If we expect to be supported, we must be willing to support.

The best cooperate and collaborate; the rest compete or compromise. A popular exercise for trainers is to draw a line on the floor with a participant on each side. The trainer then instructs that the purpose of the exercise is to convince the other, without force, to cross the line. What ensues are a range of negotiating tactics and techniques, from bribery to threats.

The simplest solution is usually the least used. That is to say, "If you cross the line, so will I." Rather than compromising or competing, the win/win solution is achieved through collaboration.

To improve your partnerships, consider how you can enrich the rewards for the other person and yourself simultaneously. Look for creative solutions that allow both partners or all team members to "win." Collaboration takes more time and creativity, but the improved outcomes build stronger, more loyal and profitable relationships.

7. Acknowledge and appreciate

One of the greatest self-help authors of all time was Og Mandino who wrote (among others) *The Greatest Salesman in the World* and *The Greatest Secret In the World*. One of my favorites is *A Better Way to Live*. In it, he offers 17 principles for a fulfilling life of exceeding success. One of those principles is "Treat each person you meet as if it were their last day on earth."

8. Practice the art of the small gesture

While working with a client on the west coast, we discovered that we were both avid auto enthusiasts. My client asked if I read a certain magazine that covered the automobile world. At that time I'd never heard of the publication. He suggested that I subscribe. The next day he handed me a subscription card to the magazine he had suggested. He had gone home the night before and removed a subscription card from one of his copies to bring to me. While a small gesture, it was significant. It demonstrated something to me about my client, and proved his concern for me.

When George Bush (George W.'s dad) became director of the CIA, he shook hands with every employee in the building, thus demonstrating his respect for and interest in every person on the team. Small gestures mean a lot in relationship building.

9. Stay grounded

Be with people, not above them. While this sounds obvious, sometimes our position, title or appearance can make it difficult for others to relate to us.

When I served as national president of the FFA organization, I spoke at many local chapter banquets. It was one of my favorite activities. I worked very hard to give a great speech, but in retrospect I believe that my speaking skills weren't what made me a hit with the chapters. Here's an example of what I really think mattered:

I would arrive earlier in the day as the final preparations were being made for the big event. Often the banquet was held in the high school auditorium or gym. As members scrambled to set up chairs, I would loosen my tie and take off my jacket and give them a hand. The reaction was often visible. A member couldn't believe that the national president was doing manual labor right alongside them. They were most appreciative.

I don't know this for certain, but I suspect that most of those members don't remember much if anything of what I said that night. But I imagine there are one or two members who remember that the national president helped them set up chairs.

Listen to words, but believe in actions.

---

10. Become a master of communication

"The belief that communication has been accomplished is one of mankind's oldest illusions."

- George Bernard Shaw

Within that admonition lies one of the great challenges the best face in getting better. So much of current success and future potential is contingent upon our ability to communicate effectively; to assure that others have not only heard what we said but understood what we meant. An even greater challenge occurs when we don't know what we mean or want when we begin the communication process.

Improving communication is not about communicating more; it's about communicating better.

"There may be no single thing more important in our efforts to achieve meaningful work and fulfilling relationships than to learn to practice the art of communication."

- Max DePree

Research by Pitney Bowes, Gallup and the Institute for the Future indicates that 70% of Fortune 1000 workers feel overwhelmed by the growing number of messages they receive—an average of 190 messages each day, most of them requiring some form of response. These include, on average, 52 phone messages, 30 email messages and 22 voicemail messages.

Language is the software of the mind. Words shape thoughts, and thoughts determine behavior. When a poor communicator fails to get a promotion, make the sale or rally the troops to march, it is easy to understand. Use words poorly—lack the power of persuasive communication—and you'll be forever limited in the results you achieve.

Improving communication is not about communicating more; it's about communicating better.

There are several distinctive differences between the best—and those who keep improving—and the rest—those content with the status quo. One of the most important distinctions is this: the best sell while the rest tell. If you want to better your best, you need to master the art of persuasion.

Words like "selling" or "sales" often have a negative connotation.

Today, that negative image is undeserved rap. There will always be unscrupulous people in every profession, and there will always be those who communicate manipulatively for personal gain at another's success. But that isn't what selling is about.

The most precise definition I've ever heard is that selling is helping people make decisions that are good for them.

The best know that their product, services and ideas must compete in the marketplace. The best work hard to provide superior quality and value. But even that isn't enough. No matter how good a product, service or idea, they still have to be sold. Otherwise, they'll be lost in the clutter and confusion of a noisy marketplace.

In an age of unlimited information, suggests Stan Davis, attention is the scarcest resource. That's why selling is of tantamount importance if you want to better your best.

The best communicators have to capture attention. They also have to deal with skepticism. So many listeners have "heard it all," that they've become jaded. Legitimate messages compete with junk mail, junk e-mail, and junk conversation.

Add to those challenges the advent of new communication technologies.

After college, I began my business career in sales and marketing. I started as an account executive selling direct marketing services. I represented a fine company with some of the best direct marketing programs in the marketplace. I enjoyed excellent rapport with the business people I called on. I was a smooth and accomplished presenter. I dressed well and worked hard. I had only one problem: very few people bought anything from me. This can be a serious impediment to advancing in a sales career.

The best communicators may be impressive, but more importantly, they influence through their words, appearance and communication skills. There is a difference between "impressing" and "influencing." Impressing someone changes what they think of you. Influencing changes what they do because of you. If you really want to upgrade your relationships, personal and professional, you'll need to master the art of persuasive communication. The next chapter tells you how.

The best communicators influence through their words, appearance and communication skills.

7

Communicate

"Example is not the main thing in persuading others, it's the only thing."

– Albert Schweitzer

The Keys to Masterful Communication

This chapter on communication could easily be titled "Relate—Part Two," a continuation or expansion of the concepts presented in Chapter Six. At the most basic level of communication, we exchange words. And when we really communicate, a lot more than mere words make the journey between people. Ideas, thoughts, feelings, the entire realm of human expression can be exchanged if we just know how to relate. Note the key word "exchange," for that's the benchmark of genuine relating. It's a two-way street that begins with effective communication—when both parties focus on the needs of their listener.

We make that me-to-you and you-to-me journey by mastering the art of persuasive communication. Here are 12 steps that will show you the way.

1. Communicate more congruently

The best know they are part of the message; that there must be a congruency between what they say, how they say it and who they are. Who you are is more powerful than what you say. People will watch what you do while they hear what you say. If there is a disconnect, more often than not, they will "hear" the behavior.

The early followers of St. Francis Assisi wanted to know what to do when they took to the streets. "Preach the gospel at all times," St. Francis advised. "If necessary, use words."

People are more persuaded by what they see than by what they hear.

2. Communicate more colorfully

To better your best at communicating, tell better stories. The primary communication tool of Jesus Christ was stories, or parables. He didn't lecture on dull points of theology. He brought his principles to life by telling stories that his listeners could relate to. He translated the abstract into the concrete by using stories.

One reason why stories are such a powerful communication tool is that they are mental coat pegs. Over the years, I've asked previous audience members what they remembered about the presentation they heard me make. Almost without exception, they remember the stories I told. Once I am able to get them talking about the stories they recall, they quickly remember some of the key points that story illustrated.

Tell better stories.

---

3. Communicate more purposely

Powerful communication creates the intended outcome. All communication has effect. Communication changes things. The best communication changes things the way we intend. It is purposeful. The best know what they want to accomplish before they begin a phone call, meeting or speech.

When I was in the publishing industry, I spent lots of time on the phone both prospecting for new clients as well as servicing and selling existing ones. I learned early on the power of identifying my call objectives before I dialed the phone. I would write out each of the items I intended to cover—what I wanted to accomplish—and check them off as the conversation progressed.

4. Communicate more overtly

Sanborn's Law: people lack imagination. If you really want your message to get heard, be overt, not covert.

It is a mistake to think that if we just give people enough information, they'll know what they should do or what we'd like them to do. Effective communication is intended to create a desired outcome. A clear and simple call to action increases greatly the likelihood of getting that result. An employee cannot be expected to achieve results that the boss cannot explain to them. You must be able to clarify the specific outcome desired if you hope to achieve it.

If you really want your message to be heard, be overt, not covert.

---

5. Communicate more creatively

The predictable is boring. Why is a joke funny? It's because there is always a surprise in the ending. What makes people want to listen? The potential of the surprising or the unusual. If the listener thinks they know what you're going to say, he or she completes the thought for you, even if the conclusion they draw is wrong.

"Why lie? I need a drink," says the honest (and creative) panhandler.

Creativity is an important factor in communication. People tend to discount the familiar; they've "heard it all before." Even when all they've heard before is true, it fails to capture their attention and interest.

Creativity is a new angle on an old subject. When the communicator takes a slightly different view, the listener is confronted with the unexpected. That is what captures their attention. Only once you've gotten their attention can you begin to persuade.

6. Communicate more concisely

The best communicators encapsulate big ideas in little packages. According to Joe Shafran, president of a talk-show placement agency, the sound byte has shrunk from three minutes in 1948 to seven seconds today. That means you have little time to get an important message across. Attention really is at a premium.

Perfect your ability to use sound bytes. Before an important meeting or presentation, write out the three most important points you hope to make. Then craft them into sound bytes of less than 10 words without losing the main message. The best go a step further and make their concisely packaged messages clever and otherwise memorable. It does little good to make a point if listeners can't remember it.

The best communicators encapsulate big ideas in little packages.

---

7. Ask for feedback

For bettering your best communications, feedback is the "breakfast of champions."

The only way you can know that you've been successful in conveying a message is when you hear the listener affirm what you've said in their own words. The best thrive on feedback. They solicit it and they give it. According to Ferdinand Fournie, 50% of performance problems are related to feedback—employees don't know how well or how badly they are doing.

Unfortunately, few people understand the substantive difference between feedback and criticism.

If someone offers constructive criticism, I ask for feedback instead. While the focus of most criticism tends to be on the person, feedback focuses on the performance. I don't want to know what you think of me—I may not be able nor even want to change who I am—but I am very interested in what you think about how I did.

I define feedback as information that can be used to improve performance. The message of positive feedback is what you did right and should keep doing. The message of negative feedback is something that is less than effective; you should either stop doing it or do it differently.

To the degree that you can separate the person from the performance, you can be soft on the person and tough on the performance. Most people respond very positive to information they can use to improve. Similarly, most people respond poorly to what they perceive as attacks on themselves.

As the speed of communication has accelerated, too often it's quality has disintegrated. While it is important to be concise, a good rule of thumb is this: the less time we have to prepare and communicate a message, the less likely it will achieve its purpose. Misunderstandings are often caused by time-compression.

Few people understand the substantive difference between feedback and criticism.

---

8. Communicate more tactfully

Practice being tactful and diplomatic. You can't always tell people what they want to hear, but you can always tell them in such a way that they'll be willing to listen.

Often communicators confuse "telling the truth" with being "brutally honest." If powerful communication is designed to create an intended outcome, unless that outcome is alienating the listener, a master communicator knows it is important to be honest without being brutal. Hurt and defensive people aren't cooperative.

You can't always tell people what they want to hear, but you can always tell them in such a way that they'll be willing to listen.

---

9. Listen better

It takes focus to be an effective communicator.

Focus brings intensity to our efforts. So, too, does focus bring intensity to our communication. Master communicators learn to block out or eliminate distractions. You know when talking with them that you have their complete attention; for that period, you are the most important person in the world.

Most people speak at a rate of 135-175 words per minute, but most of us can comprehend at a rate of 3-400 words per minute. This gap between speaking and listening comprehension is one of the most common barriers to effective communication. Our attention begins to wander and the thought we come up with to take up the slack in mental stimulation often prevents us from hearing what the other person is really saying.

When it comes to verbal communication, listening is essential to learning. You can't help someone make a decision that is good for them if you don't know what they want, need and desire. It isn't enough to be able to present your message persuasively; the best communicators understand the importance of listening.

10. Communicate less seriously

Some people like to be challenged and stimulated with provocative ideas. Even more people also like to be entertained. But if you want to win people over, learn how to make them laugh. Using humor is one of the most powerful tools of the best communicators. They know if you win someone's heart, their head isn't far behind.

11. Communicate less perfectly

"My album is full of pops, clicks, buzzes, and hums, notes I don't quite get to, notes I miss completely—but it's all part of being human. The perfection is in the imperfection."

- Jyoti Mishra (a.k.a. White Town)
Recording Artist

A friend of mine proved this point many years ago. After spending a year perfecting his speaking skills as the national officer of a large youth organization, he returned to his large college campus. He decided to run for student body president. The problem was his perfection. When addressing the students in the course of the campaign, he was perceived as too polished and his speaking skills too perfect. His ability was working against him. His solution was to write small mistakes and flaws into his speeches. In effect, he detuned his presentation skills to make himself more human to the student body. He won the election.

Former presidential speech write Peggy Noonan is correct when she says, "A winning eagerness, a surprising awkwardness, and ingenuous lack of perfection— these are endearing things to see in a successful person." To be influential, the best communicators are less than perfect, because this allows them to be seen as the human beings they really are.

12. Involve your listener

In his excellent book *Mastery*, George Leonard shared this important point: "The best teacher is not necessarily the one who gives the most polished lectures, but rather the one who has discovered how to involve each student actively in the process of learning."

Good communicators find ways to involve listeners. In professional selling, the sale pro asks a prospective customer to fill-in a brief survey to identify needs. A speaker uses group involvement in his or her presentation to drive a point home. A parent shows her small son how to use art supplies then asks him to try it himself while she watches and offers suggestions.

The best communication is active rather than passive. To be better, find more ways to involve listeners.

13. Present more powerfully

A powerful public speaker possesses one of the greatest tools of influence of all. If communicating powerfully one-on-one is helpful to bettering your best, being able to influence groups leverages that skill dramatically. The topic of powerful public speaking could fill an entire book, but I'll close this chapter with six simple ideas that, if applied, will make you a better speaker. (While the following points are literally sound bytes, they illustrate how much information can be communicated quickly and concisely.)

- It isn't enough to have a message. It must be your message. What is it about your topic that is important to you? That is where your uniqueness lies. When you discover your message, you also release your passion. I have found that education is usually best delivered on the wings of entertainment.

- At the beginning of every speech, your primary challenge is to break preoccupation. Each audience member is preoccupied with their own thoughts and concerns. A powerful, attention-grabbing beginning is critical.
- People don't remember your points, they remember your illustrations. If they can remember the story, then they will be able to remember the point or lesson that the story teaches. As in interpersonal communication, stories are like mental coat-pegs: a place for listeners to hang ideas.
- End with a call to action. Make it clear what you would like your audience to do as a result of your presentation. Be clear on what they should do, not just what they should think.
- The primary reason why speakers fail is lack of preparation. Practice may not make perfect, but it does make one better. Enough practice makes one great. If you're serious about becoming an effective public speaker, join Toastmasters International. They'll be listed in your phone book or just ask around.

It isn't enough to have a message.
It must be your message.

From Me to You

Approximately 22,000 members of the FFA congregate each year in Kansas City for their annual convention.

In 1978-79 I served as national president of that youth organization. The culmination of my year of leadership would be my retiring address which would be presented at the convention.

The executive director of the Ohio FFA and one of my mentors was Dr. Earl F. Kantner. Whenever I had an important decision to make, I often bounced ideas around with "Doc." I told him that I was considering titling my retiring address "A Part of Me." The premise was simple: as I had traveled and met with FFA members for the past year, those people and experiences had become an important part of me.

"Well, I think the angle is all wrong. Why not call it 'A Part of You.' That way the focus will be on the members, not on you. It's always more important when you focus on the listener rather than the speaker; more powerful if you go from 'me' to 'you.'"

He was right. I called my speech "A Part of You" and it really seemed to resonate with the audience. And I still got my point across, but the message had become more universal: we all, in some way, become part of each other when we interact significantly.

People are more interested in themselves than they are in the speaker—or the salesperson or the doctor or the bank officer. You can still communicate the message you desire if you remember to make your listeners the center of attention. All it takes is going from "me" to "you."

"It's always more important when you focus on the listener rather than the speaker; more powerful if you go from 'me' to 'you.'"

8

Adapt: Conquering Change

"Take change by the hand or it will seize you by the throat."

– Winston Churchill

Change is one of the things in life that we don't (and can't) control. Experts estimate that 94% of the changes we face are imposed by other people and circumstances. If there's one thing that's constant in life, it's that the world is always changing. Just when you've reached your quarterly sales goal, your boss raises it for the next quarter. It's tough to keep improving when the world around you is changing so fast.

For most people, particularly those of us in the fast-paced business world, change is about the only thing you can count on! No one is immune. If you don't like the change that is occurring around you, you can't escape it by changing jobs or changing addresses. Change is an inescapable circumstance of life. To better your best in any aspect of your life—you must learn how to deal with and make the most of change.

Chances are you haven't been taught how to change. My informal research with corporate audiences suggests that less than 20% of Americans have ever had any kind of education or training on managing change.

At a biological level, change and adaptation are normal and natural. At a psychological level, change is much harder.

Dr. Frank Pittman, writing in *Psychology Today*, said, "The world is changing so rapidly that people don't have to be mentally ill to be out of their minds some of the time, behaving inappropriately much of the time and a little bit disoriented all of the time." Some might believe, "We have met the enemy, and the enemy is change."

It's No Longer "Back to Normal," but "Forward to Normal"

I meet people daily who believe that if they just hunker down and stand their ground, someday things will get "back to normal." The best understand this new reality of change: the past is incapable of explaining the future. Normal lies ahead, not behind. Things will never be the same again. They look ahead and anticipate what normal will look like if they successfully deal with change.

Language is the software of the mind. Change your programming by changing your use of words and phrases. Start thinking and talking in terms of "forward to normal."

We are not in control of the majority of the changes that affect us. Some changes are initiated by us; others are imposed by others or by circumstance. The best know they can't always count on being "proactive" to determine which changes will impact them. They are as skilled in dealing with imposed change as they are initiating beneficial change and they make the most of it.

It's no longer "back to normal," but "forward to normal"

Change Has Changed

Today change is revolutionary and it isn't always enough to adjust. Those most skilled at dealing with change know that often full-blown transformation is necessary. They know that the very nature of change is different, unlike it's ever been.

What specifically has changed about change? There are three primary differences:

Speed: World events are beamed into our homes as they occur. Worldwide communication is instantaneous. Businesses are created, expanded, diversified, bought, sold and restructured overnight.

Magnitude: Because of the velocity of technological innovation, changes today are larger and more dramatic than those of the past.

Complexity: We live in an interconnected and interdependent world. Change often requires the mutual cooperation of others to be successfully resolved.

Resistance to Change—Part of Being Human

Unfortunately, it's our human nature to resist change, to stay within our comfort zones and avoid the hard work that change requires. Tackling change is a risk that we're often reluctant to take, even when we're sure that the result will be an improvement for our personal or professional lives.

Just Do It!

I believe the reason most of us don't change is that we don't focus on the key that underlies all change: DOING! In fact, if we don't DO, effective and lasting change will never happen. Corporate America loves to study and analyze—but rarely does it DO anything differently. Companies send people to classes, have high-level executive meetings, allocate funding, and talk a lot about change. But rarely do they get beyond the talking stage. Even though your goal might seem miles away, it will get closer only when you take that first step of DOING.

I believe the reason most of us don't change is that we don't focus on the key that underlies all change: DOING!

Do the Right Things

There's a saying that goes, "To accomplish nothing, attempt everything." The danger is in bursting out of the blocks in your enthusiasm to do without a focused plan of the RIGHT THINGS to do. Once you've decided to do, make a list of your options.

Say, for example, your boss has just increased your sales goals for the next quarter. You're ready to tackle the new challenge. But first, make a list of all the different ways you can accomplish an increase in sales, such as asking existing clients for referrals, improving your prospecting or beginning a direct mail program. Of those actions you can take, decide which ones are the MVP—Most Valuable & Profitable—ones to take. Those are the RIGHT THINGS to do. Then you're set to go with a clear focus.

Do the Right Things Consistently

Pursuing more sales one afternoon of every quarter probably won't result in significant increases. Even if you're doing the right things, you must do them CONSISTENTLY, or lasting and effective change will elude you.

Don't leave it to chance—manage your schedule, and be sure you have set aside adequate time. Awareness and discipline keep unimportant time-eaters on the back burner so that we can accomplish those things that are truly worthwhile. The longer you perform a task, the more efficient you'll become, and the less time it will absorb.

No matter what you want to change, it takes doing. It takes doing the right things. It takes doing the right things consistently!

From Inhibitor to Agent

"What we want," my client was explaining, "Is for our managers to be change agents rather than change inhibitors."

If there is something that the best have in common when it comes to change, it's that they anticipate what they can, embrace what is inevitable and initiate what is desirable. Like an akido martial artist, they use the energy of change to work for them rather than resist it.

If there is something that the best have in common when it comes to change, it's that they anticipate what they can, embrace what is inevitable and initiate what is desirable.

How to Upgrade Through Change

The discomfort of the known is often preferred to the potential benefits of the unknown. We prefer the familiar over any disruption of our equilibrium.

When you consider an improvement of any kind, you realize that it always requires you change what you're doing before you'll experience the benefit of accomplishment. Let's look at how the best deal with change.

1. Change before pain and survival necessitate it

Everyone eventually changes, or they disappear. When an individual or organization only change because they are threatened by a existing rival or new upstart, they find themselves behind the eight ball. That's probably why the late Mike Walsh, former CEO of Tenneco said, "In my opinion, there are two kinds of businesses in the United States: those that are heading for the cliff and know it, and those that are heading the same way but don't know it. Our advantage is, we know it."

2. Let change stretch and grow you

Even the best can't control or anticipate all the changes that confront them. They realize, however, that change always represents the opportunity for growth.

Author Don Nicholl, in his profound book *Holiness*, summarizes those opportunities for growth from a spiritual perspective. He says, "...the exhilarating truth that every single moment of our daily life, every experience, at whatever time and at whatever place, can serve, and is meant to serve, as spiritual exercise—so long as we, by our attitude, recognize that the experience is meant for that purpose...no experience is wasted."

3. Enjoy the increased community and teamwork change can create

Change can create community and teamwork.

Departments that once feuded over turf issues suddenly cooperate when faced with the threat of a new competitor. Entire companies threatened with layoffs if they can't meet their numbers become supercharged to achieve those objectives to protect each other's jobs.

Some of the best team leaders I have observed have used change as a way to gel previously uncooperative team members within their organizations.

Seven Keys to Mastering Change

A trademark of those who keep getting better is that they focus on what needs to be done, rather than how they feel. Following are seven skills for becoming a master of change.

1. Practice the 3A's of change: Anticipate, Accept and Act

Anticipate what you can

"Prediction is difficult, especially when it is about the future."

– Yogi Berra

Predicting the future is easy. Predicting it correctly is very difficult. Some change can be anticipated. Much change cannot. An attentiveness to what's changing in the world around you—your community, business and industry—is helpful. Search for information that will help you anticipate key changes and prepare accordingly. But understand that even the best at anticipation are going to be less than 100% accurate, both about the changes that will affect them, as well as the correct actions to take.

Predicting the future is easy. Predicting it correctly is very difficult. Accept what you can't anticipate or avoid.

ACCEPT WHAT YOU CAN'T ANTICIPATE OR AVOID

The sooner you move past resisting change, the sooner you'll be able to deploy your considerable resources in responding to the change.

ACT ACCORDINGLY

While the rest are arguing against a change, the best are acting on it. The Best Are Ready, Willing and Able. Here's what that means:

- You're ready when you've identified the change and understand the implications it has for your success.
- You're willing when you accept responsibility for making the appropriate response to that change.
- You're able when you are capable of dealing with the change because you have the skills and motivation necessary for doing what needs to be done.

2. How you feel about change doesn't have to determine what you do about changing

Change masters are expert planners. That means asking the question, What needs to happen for me to successfully deal with this change?

And the most important part of any plan is the first step. Once you've identified the first step, break the change down into bite-size pieces. One of the big secrets of change mastery is that the best conserve energy for the important life changes. They don't commit the same psychic or physical energy to every change they encounter. By prioritizing the steps to an individual change as well as the changes they encounter, they'll be better able to allocate resources effectively.

3. Work on your foundation

In a reader poll by *Futurist* magazine 84% agreed that Western culture is failing to provide a sense of meaning, belonging, purpose and a framework of values." One particularly astute woman wrote, "It is not culture's job to do this. It is our job to find it."

I agree.

The job she alluded to is the construction of a personal foundation to weather the storms of life. If it hasn't happened yet, it will. Change is going to shake you. You will be tested. Author Philip Yancey says, "You cannot suddenly fabricate foundations of strength; they must have been building all along."

The Three F's of a Strong Foundation

Your foundation for dealing with change is built upon these things: faith, family and friends.

FAITH

Faith is your belief in a power and purpose larger than yourself. In the Judeo-Christian tradition, that someone is God.

The thinking person's approach to faith is the pursuit of truth. I don't want to believe merely because it feels good; I want to believe because it is true. The challenge of faith is to seek the truth about God and know Him in a way that is not only accurate but personal. For me personally, the Bible is the greatest source of strength as I deal with change. Especially comforting is Romans 8:28 that states, "All things work together for the good of them that love God..." That scripture says that God can use all those things that happen—even the bad things—for my good. That is a central belief in my faith.

FAMILY AND FRIENDS

Change masters develop and maintain a strong support system. Your family knows, understands and supports you because of their relationship to you. Friends really include two groups: professional and personal friends. Professional friends are willing to offer advice, counsel and encouragement that will help in handling the change. These professional friends would include counselors, therapists or clergy.

Change masters develop and maintain a strong support system.

Personal friends may or may not understand your business or challenges, but are willing to listen and support you. The objective of a support group of family and friends is to assist you in dealing with change, not take responsibility for you. My friend John Crudele and I were talking about the difference between "caring" and "caretaking." Caring is healthy. Caretaking is usually not because it means we have assumed too much responsibility for someone else's life

4. Develop a perspective of optimistic realism

"Two men looked out the prison bars: one saw mud, the other stars."

So much of what happens in life is not easily categorized as simply good or bad. Change always involves some form of loss. The realist knows that simply whistling a happy tune or reciting motivational bromides aren't enough to deal with the unpleasantness and sometimes pain of change. The optimistic realist, however, is able to keep the effect of change in perspective.

No matter how difficult a circumstance or situation, there are people facing much more severe circumstances. Sometimes we should sober ourselves by looking at those who are far less fortunate to keep our own lives in perspective. When something annoying or upsetting occurred, my grandfather used to say, "It's an inconvenience, but it's not fatal." How true those words often are.

Another way to keep change in perspective is to take a long-term view. Five years from now, will the changes you are facing still seem dramatic? In 10 years? By taking a macro view of change, rather than a micro view, change is often seen as far less significant.

Change can shock us into doing what really needs to be done in our lives. To be optimistic requires confidence in your ability to deal successfully with change. The best relive victories, while the rest relive defeats.

One of the best ways to feel better about yourself and build confidence is to focus on those times in the past when you've been successful. Relive all those situations in the past where the change seemed insurmountable and yet you succeeded.

Change can shock us into doing what really needs to be done in our lives.

---

5. Look for the lessons

Most of us would not choose to grow if life didn't force us to—we would choose only easy growth. I believe God signs us up for the courses that we wouldn't voluntarily take.

There is almost always a lesson in even the most painful and unsuccessful changes. Learn to look for it. Like getting tiny pieces of precious metals extracted from iron ore, it may require painstaking effort, but it's worth it.

Most of us would not choose to grow if life didn't force us to.

---

6. Laugh about it

"A sense of humor is the ability to take yourself lightly and find humor even in tense situations."

– Scott Freidman

A Burke Marketing Research survey found that 84% of personnel directors felt employees with a sense of humor do a better job than those lacking that quality. Could it be that humor makes us more change resilient as well?

Even companies can benefit from using humor to soften the hard challenges they face. At Digital Equipment Corp, which slashed 20% of its work force in the last two years, the new E-Mail riddle is: "What's the difference between DEC and Jurassic Park? One is a high-tech theme park full of dinosaurs. The other is a Steven Spielberg movie."

As a child I learned this wise old adage: "God gave us a sense of humor because He knew there would be problems we couldn't solve on our own."

God gave us a sense of humor because He knew there would be problems we couldn't solve on our own.

---

7. Encourage others

The best know that one of the most effective ways to manage personal change is to encourage others and to assist them in coping with the changes they face. Why?

First, the success of colleagues and coworkers—your team—impacts you own success. Encouragement strengthens your network.

Secondly, when we encourage others we are often encouraged ourselves. We can benefit from encouragement by giving it away. By helping others keep their perspective and strengthening their resolve, we benefit from the message as well.

Thirdly, encouraging others prevents dangerous self-absorption which saps our strength by focusing on the problem, rather than looking for the solution. By breaking our self-absorption, we can move past how we feel to what we need to do.

Finally, encouraging others increases the chance for receiving support in the future when we really need it. We get back what we give out. To receive more love, be more loving. To receive encouragement, encourage others.

Conclusion

Change itself has changed. The best don't resist or even passively accept change, they embrace it. They are masters at doing what needs to be done when a change is imposed, and they often initiate change—for themselves and their organizations—when they want to move ahead of their competition.

Change is an inside job. Although the circumstances of change are external, the best have developed the skills of personal change mastery that allow them to change faster and better than the rest.

9

Discipline: The Keys to Self-Mastery

"Strong lives are motivated by dynamic purpose."

– Kenneth Hildebrand

If you know what you want out of life, you can almost always figure out a way to get it. All it takes is determination and drive. Successful and fulfilled people live lives by design, not by default. Going from where you are to where you want to be is the process of change. What it takes to get there is self-mastery.

Knowing where you want to end up is the challenge of personal leadership. The best live lives by design, not by default.

Why Get Up?

For more than a decade I've asked audiences the question, "Why do you get out of bed in the morning?" The most frequent responses are always the same. "I have to get up, I've got to...." I call this the "vague sense of obligation" response. The idea is that getting up is required if one expects to make a living and take care of themselves and family. Fact is that most people don't have to get out of bed in the morning. If they chose to just lay there, neither their lives nor the world at large would be dramatically impacted. Perhaps he or she would be a little behind the next day and have to catch up. Meetings would be missed and appointments would be rescheduled and the other spouse might have to pick a child up after school, but nothing truly terrible would happen. "I have to" is not a compelling reason to get out of bed.

The next most common response is humorous but insightful. "Because I have to go to the bathroom!"

Does this explain a lot about your coworkers? You: "Why'd you come into the office this morning?" Colleague: "Well, I got up about 6:30 to go to the bathroom and figured as long as I was up I might as well head into the office and see what's going on."

More people, it seems, are motivated by their bladders than by their beliefs!

Many years ago Dr. Charles Garfield did seminal research on peak performance. He identified six attributes shared by peak performers regardless of profession. Chief among them is a sense of purpose. They are powered by knowing not only what they do, but why they do it. His research has withstood the test of time.

Helen Keller must have felt a similar excitement in her life when she said "To me, life is a daring adventure." In stark contrast, Henry David Thoreau reminded us that most people live lives of "quiet desperation." If there is a pop quiz at the end of life, here are three questions that I don't think will be included: Who did you work for? What was your title? How much did they pay you? I think one question you could reasonably expect is, "Of all the things you could have spent your lifetime doing, why'd you chose to do what you did?"

From Obligation to Opportunity

Several years ago, I too was close to premature flame-out. I was traveling nearly non-stop. I wasn't having much fun and I found it increasingly more difficult to give people the attention and consideration they deserved. When the phone rang, I didn't want to answer it. I wanted to smash it. I wasn't carrying the weight of the world on my shoulders, but it did feel like a rather large moon. I knew that soon I would be experiencing the repercussions of others' frustration with me. (When you aren't having much fun, rest assured that neither are your clients, colleagues, friends, or family!) I wondered, "How can anyone live happily and lead effectively with so many oppressive obligations?"

When I finally stopped my frenetic pace long enough to slow down and look for an answer, I was struck with an insight. The people who change the world—their companies, communities, and families—rarely act from a sense of oppressive obligation. In fact, the people we call "true leaders" almost always act from a sense of incredible opportunity. They don't change the world because they have to. They change the world because they want to.

The people who change the world rarely act from a sense of oppressive obligation.

I don't think Mother Teresa woke up even one morning and complained, "Oh, Lord, not more lepers!" She did some of the hardest work on the planet, and she seemed to have more fun than we who sit in plush, air-conditioned offices. How can that be?

It's a matter of perspective. When we feel harried and pressured, we tend to look at our circumstances as oppressive obligations. On the other hand, those few who live happily and lead effectively view such circumstances as incredible opportunities. To put it simply: Leaders frame their lives differently.

When I learned from the example of the world's great leaders and re-framed my work and life, things immediately turned around. I began to see circumstances as opportunities rather than obligations, and it has made all the difference. When the phone rings now, I respond differently. I view each call as an opportunity to serve, earn, influence, network, learn, encourage, or teach. The difference isn't in the caller or the purpose for the call; the difference is in my response.

As you read this, perhaps you're facing dire circumstances. Foreclosure may threaten, a primary relationship may be on the brink of disaster, or you may be wondering how you're going to put food on the table. I would never make light of such serious situations, but—and please think about this carefully—even in the worst circumstance lies an opportunity. It is the opportunity to overcome, to save, to improve. I know many highly successful individuals who have faced similar situations, and worse. But meeting the challenge to overcome and learn from these situations has, without fail, greatly enriched their lives. In their darkest hour, they saw and pursued that faint glimmer of light called opportunity.

I keep a sticky note over my desk. On it are three words: "Obligation or Opportunity." That simple sentiment represents one of the most important choices I make every day, every hour. Like you, I want to make a positive impact on the world around me. I want to add to the lives of others, not just pass by them unnoticed. I want to be confident that my efforts do more than earn a living, that they help create a better life for myself, my family, and the clients I serve. And now I realize that the chance to accomplish this goal is not an obligation, but the greatest opportunity of all.

Who Is in the Driver's Seat?

Jack Welch co-authored the book, *Take Control of Your Destiny or Someone Else Will.* While the book recounts what made GE the powerhouse company it is today, Welch's advice applies just as aptly to our personal lives.

While the best are masters of circumstance, the rest are mastered by circumstance. Phil is an example. Today he is 34 years old. As a child, he loved music, but his parents told him he could never make a living playing the piano. He got a degree in business. He married Joan during their senior year at college. They had job offers in different cities. Phil decided to go with Joan so she could get a position as an accountant, but the job market where her new employer was located was tight, so he went back to school to get his teaching certificate.

This was something his friends encouraged him to do. He taught business at the high school level for several years. He was considering teaching piano part-time when they had their first child. He thought piano lessons would be disruptive, so he postponed the idea. Thirteen years out of college, and Phil makes decent money teaching a subject he doesn't really enjoy to students who really don't care.

You could say that Phil is a pragmatist—"you gotta' do what you gotta' do"—and to a degree that's true. The tragedy is that practically every major decision in Phil's life was made by someone else. The path was set early on, and before he knew it, Phil's life was no longer his own. Maybe we each recognize a little of ourselves in that story. So what's the alternative?

While the best are masters of circumstance, the rest are mastered by circumstance.

When I learned to fly, I learned about the aviation acronym "PIC" which stands for "pilot in command." Typically, it's the person who's flying in the left seat. If there are two people in the cockpit, it's critically important to know who is in charge, especially if there's an emergency situation.

The best are PIC—the "person in command"—of their lives. The rest tend to be OIC—others in command—abdicating responsibility for their lives to outside forces. People who take charge of their own lives are ultimately much better equipped to be of service to family, friends and others. They consider the input of others as important, but "in addition to" rather than "in place of" their own dreams and desires.

The best accept the responsibility that no other human being is more responsible for them than they are. To be true to others begins by being true to yourself.

Competency Without Character Is Dangerous

I'm often asked what gets people to follow leaders. Where do leaders get credibility? I believe there are two primary sources of credibility: competence and character. Competence is mastery of what you do. Character is the reality of who you are. Both are necessary for effective leadership.

The best are those who have not chosen to worship competency over character.

No child, employee or citizen should ever have to choose between competency and character in their leadership. It is necessary for leaders to understand that being great at what you do without being good at who you are is a tragedy. The great insight here is this: what we do, how well we perform and the material gains that we enjoy flow out of who we are. Character and competency are the driving forces of not only credibility but greatness.

There are two primary sources of credibility: Competence is mastery of what you do; Character is the reality of who you are. Both are necessary for effective leadership.

Transform Your Attitude

The best choose and develop their attitude; the rest let circumstances develop their attitude.

T. D. Jakes says, "You must eat from the garden of your own thoughts. So don't grow anything you don't want to eat." One of the greatest battles we face in mastering self involve attitude. Attitude is an internal feeling expressed in external behaviors. Attitude creates perspective or "spin." It determines how we interpret the world around us.

The best have discovered that attitude is always a choice. If you have a fatalistic attitude, that is a choice you've made. Circumstance has not made that choice for you. If you are known for an enthusiastic attitude, that is because you have made a different choice.

Several years ago I heard a speaker named Jim Pelly. Jim talked about the challenges of travel. His comments impacted me greatly. He said, "If you are a professional speaker and you don't like to travel, you have a choice. Either choose to enjoy it, or quit doing it." I thought about that. Up until then, I had chosen to complain about it. Of course verbalizing my displeasure only added to my displeasure, not to mention the displeasure of others. That was the day I chose to change my attitude about travel.

The best focus on the positive;
the rest water the weeds.

My friend James Ray says "If you're a gardener, you know you don't have to water the weeds. They seem to grow on their own, despite your best efforts. The good plants—the fruits and vegetables—they need your attention if you want them to grow. A positive attitude is the same way."

The best focus on the positive; the rest water the weeds. There is nothing inappropriate with acknowledging or accepting the difficulties, challenges and imperfections of life. But to focus on them is the equivalent of cultivating them. A positive attitude is attained through the careful cultivation of the best thinking and highest ideals.

From the PIT to the TOP

Attitude affects how we react to what happens to us and how we interact with the world around us. Our attitude towards our efforts to succeed and improve either helps or hinders us. In the study of those with a positive attitude, there are three distinct differences. To remember those distinctions, I've coined the acronyms PIT and TOP. To transform your attitude means going from the PIT of a negative attitude to the TOP of a positive attitude.

When something unfortunate occurs, you can frame the event as permanent or temporary. A negative attitude frames such setbacks as permanent with language like, "that's always the case" or "I never get any breaks." The transformed attitude says, "stuff happens, no big deal, I'll win next time."

Our attitude towards our efforts to succeed and improve either helps or hinders us.

The second choice is how to attribute cause. The negativist believes the problem is internal. "I'm flawed" or "I can't do anything right" places the blame internally. They're not taking responsibility; they're taking blame. The positive person looks for the outside cause of the failure. When they locate what went wrong or needs to be done differently, they can address it.

Finally, the negativist feels trapped. After all, the problem is permanent and internal. The positive person believes the problem is temporary and caused by an outside event. They move ahead with a plan to deal with it.

PIT TO TOP THINKING

Permanent	**T**emporary
Internal Factor	**O**utside Factor
Trapped	**P**lan

Master Your Moods

Five simple words are the mantra of the unsuccessful: "I don't feel like it." Whenever you utter these words, you've just made your mood the ruler of you life. According to the University of Michigan, most people spend about three days of every 10 trying to shake off bad moods. Judging from the behavior of many, they aren't successful in doing so.

The best control their moods; the rest are controlled by their moods.

Honest evaluation of self always uncovers blemishes, imperfections, weaknesses or worse. None of us need to be discouraged by these faults, but all of us need to address and overcome those that we can.

You are known, for the most part, by what you do. Your outward behaviors and interactions tell others who you are. When you let your moods determine those behaviors and interactions, you allow yourself to be mastered by those moods. Like Moses, you and I need to struggle against our faults and weaknesses, rather than succumb to them.

Practice What You Preach

A woman took her young son to see Mahatma Gandhi. She asked him to instruct the boy to quit eating sugar. Gandhi told her to come back in three days. When she returned three days later, Gandhi told the boy, "Stop eating sugar." The woman was puzzled. "Why didn't you tell him to stop eating sugar the first time we visited you?" "I couldn't tell him that," Gandhi explained, "because three days ago I too was eating sugar."

It is easy to believe and even instruct. Practicing those beliefs and instructions are much more difficult. Discipline is the bridge between belief and behavior. My own definition of discipline is the ability to do what needs to be done despite how one feels about doing it

You don't get recognized and rewarded for what you feel like. You get rewarded and recognized for what you do.

Gain the Edge of Extra Effort

"When I was a young man, I observed that nine out of ten things I did were failures. I didn't want to be a failure so I did ten times more work."

– George Bernard Shaw

Ever heard the old cliche' that selling is a numbers game? It's not true. Selling is a numbers-and-skill game. Results = Activity (number of contacts) x Skill (ability to convert those contacts to sales). All the activity in the world won't pay off with much results without the pre-requisite skills.

The reverse is also true. Highly refined skills produce results only when applied. But there is one area of our lives completely within our control: our ability to work. In the new millennium, one old colloquialism that will still be true: the harder you work, the luckier you get.

Choose to Be a Victor of Circumstance

"You make a choice to go forward. If you don't make that choice somewhere, you become a victim."

– Lois Benjamin

We live in a culture that seems to believe that it's not whether you win or lose, but how you place the blame. This is the essence of victim mentality. Victim mentality is about neither taking responsibility nor blame; it's about placing blame. When something bad happens, we have a phrase that was originally used in sympathy: victim of circumstance. Unfortunately, some choose the phrase as an explanation for their lives.

The best are not victims of circumstance. They are victors of circumstance. They experience setbacks and injustices, some of their own making but many undeserved. The difference is in how they respond. While you can't control everything that happens to you in life, you can always choose how you respond.

The best are not victims of circumstance. They are victors of circumstance.

Motivate Yourself

If you are a PIC (person in charge) then you need to realize that includes the responsibility of staying motivated. Don't wait for somebody else to "motivate" you. It's an inside job.

The best choose to do those things that help them become better. Searching out good programs of skill development, education and/or motivation become a priority for those committed to infinite improvement. But motivating yourself includes more than listening to speakers, taking classes or attending seminars.

In a survey of 435 CEO's from American's fastest-growing privately held companies, entrepreneurs were asked to select their favorite technique for staying motivated. 63.9% said finding a new challenge inside the business. That was the most popular response. (Inc. Mar. 98) Getting better—infinite improvement—is a primary motivator for the best.

The late Dale Earnhardt was one of the winningest drivers in NASCAR Winston Cup Racing, but winning the 1998 Daytona 500 was a special victory. In the three decades Earnhardt raced, he accumulated 70 career victories but winning the Daytona 500 had eluded him for 20 years. Although Earnhardt had won the Winston Cup title seven times, the 1998 race was his 21st attempt at winning the Daytona 500.

His victory on February 15th also broke a 59-race winless streak dating to March 1996. His fans had stood by him during the winless period. And on the way to victory lane, pit crews from virtually every team lined pit road to congratulate him, a sight rarely seen in Winston Cup racing. Like John Elway of the Super Bowl Champion Denver Broncos who had experienced the high point of his career just weeks earlier, Earnhardt was a favorite to win.

While Earnhardt's racing career was a study in perseverance and determination, it is also instructive in how to maintain a winning attitude in the face of deep discouragement. The day before the race he met a little girl in a wheelchair through the Make-A-Wish Foundation. Earnhardt described her as "tiny with a pretty voice." She took a penny from her pocket, rubbed it and gave it to him with the promise "this is going to win you the Daytona 500." He glued the penny to his dashboard and it was with him in victory lane. Said Earnhardt, "A little girl like that in a wheelchair, and life has not been good to, giving you a penny and wishing you good luck to win the Daytona 500—that's pretty special."

Don't wait for somebody else to motivate you. It's an inside job.

Create a High-Performance Lifestyle

Jack Lalayne was once asked why, in his 70's he still worked out so hard, and why he was known to like to have a good time. Lalayne's explanation: "I put a lot in so I can take a lot out." It is hard to live a high performance life in a low performance body. Nothing will prevent you from bettering your best quicker than poor health or a low performance lifestyle. Creating a high performance lifestyle isn't easy, but neither is it as hard as many assume.

Make sure that you're getting at least 30 minutes or more of moderate-intensity physical activity most days of the week. A panel convened by the Centers for Disease Control and Prevention and the American College of Sports Medicine made this recommendation in early 1994. The panel believes that adults who exercise at this level will receive significant health benefits.

Twelve-point-eight million Americans use free weights twice a week or more. That's important, because after age 25, men lose about seven pounds of muscle a decade if they don't do something to prevent it. Women lose about five pounds a decade before menopause and about ten pounds a decade after. New research shows that you can make significant improvements in muscle strength and tone without training for an hour or more three times a week. Lifting weights for only two times each week for 20-30 minutes can produce almost the same results as longer workouts three days a week. And strength training makes losing weight faster and easier.

The journal *Nature* also found that growth factors in the brain—compounds responsible for the brain's health—can be controlled by exercise. Exercisers live longer and score higher on tests of mental function. This indicates the importance of physical activity in the aging process. And yet despite these benefits, only one in every five Americans exercise regularly. Of those who don't exercise, 51% say it is because they don't have the time. If you fall into that excuse category, you owe it to yourself to make the time.

According to *LIFE* magazine (February 1998), eighty percent of all Americans are sleep deprived. We spend $2.5 billion on pocket sleep remedies and 3,000 sleep disorder clinics have sprung up in the past 15 years. Most adults need 7-8 hours of sleep to be fully rested. Most are getting significantly less. Furthermore, you cannot recoup lost sleep in a day or two. Sleep deprivation can take an extended period of time to overcome, so simply sleeping-in on the weekends is an inadequate solution.

It's also important to minimize those substances that affect your energy negatively. Caffeine, alcohol, cigarettes, and sugar can confuse the body, especially when ingested close to bedtime. Some other ideas helpful for maintaining higher energy levels: Eat more frequently and stay hydrated. Light healthy snacking—fruits, vegetables, not candy—provides the body with an ongoing source of fuel between meals. Healthy snacking between meals prevents over-eating at regular meal times.

And importantly, stay hydrated. Drink lots of water. Water plays a critical role in digestion and nutrition; you can think of it as the oil that keeps your metabolic engine lubricated.

Burn Bright, but Don't Flame-Out

For most of us, stress is inevitable. The more you attempt, the more activities you fill your life with, the more stress you will experience. The challenge isn't to avoid stress; the challenge is to manage stress. The best learn to thrive on it.

I once visited a butterfly sanctuary. The air in the enclosure was filled with some of the world's most beautiful and exotic butterflies. One of the most striking, and my personal favorite, was a large, bright blue butterfly. This particular butterfly is one of the fastest flying butterflies in the world, but it has a very short life span. The butterfly's wings collide each time they flap and when the wings wear out, the butterfly becomes vulnerable to predators. Because this one flies so fast, it's wings wear out fast as well. In the world of butterflies, the faster you fly, the faster you die.

I can offer no magic formula for determining how much stress is enough or too much for you. It is evident that if the stress in your life has become debilitating—if it is causing psychological and physiological barriers to your improvement and performance—you need either reduce it, or learn more effective strategies for dealing with it. Here is a simple question to regularly ask yourself: am I flying too fast? Are the consequences associated with your lifestyle affecting your longevity?

The challenge isn't to avoid stress; the challenge is to manage stress. The best learn to thrive on it.

A problem for achievers is that they are often the last to notice the stress they have created for themselves. They don't figure it out until a vital organ stops working or a spouse packs up the kids and furniture. Achievers often become so self-absorbed in their pursuit of improvement that they become willing to pay any price to attain it. I don't subscribe to the school of thought that says get better at any and all costs. There are some costs that aren't worth paying (and your health and relationships are primary among them).

You can't burn bright if you're burnt out.

Are You Failure-Proof?

"Many of life's failures are people who did not realize how close they were to success when they gave up."

- Thomas Edison

Let me define the difference between failing and failure. You fail when you try something and don't achieve it. You only become a failure when you quit trying. The best know that if they aren't failing, they aren't improving. This is one of the least known factors in infinite improvement. It matters not the endeavor; your willingness to try, to risk and to fail is an absolute pre-requisite to infinite improvement.

That doesn't mean you won't fail—you will fail often as you improve—but you can avoid joining the ranks of those who give up the fight and stop pursuing their dreams. Anything you attempt that you don't initially master or achieve is a stepping stone to your improvement if one or more of these four things occurs:

1) you move closer to your goals and objectives
2) you learn something in the process

3) the setback motivates you to try again
4) you accept it as proof of your resilience—you survived!

Here's the difference between failing and failure: you fail when you try something and don't achieve it. You only become a failure when you quit trying.

Conclusion

You can't master your profession, your hobby, your financial situation or anything else for that matter until you first master yourself. The best who are able to continually get better are those who above all are masters of self.

10

Execute

"No amount of insight or wisdom accounts for much, I've found, if it doesn't lead to changes in behavior."

– Tony Schwartz

What Matters Most

I felt bone weary and drained. I had just spoken for 2000 people and walked offstage at 11:45 a.m. At noon my client whisked me away for a quick lunch in the hotel restaurant. Our lunch was pleasant enough but there wasn't a moment's rest for me. We got to the meeting room of the second group of 100 that I was to address. They asked if I would sit in on the first part of the meeting. Without an opportunity to use the restroom or get a cup of coffee, I obliged. At 1:45 p.m. I was introduced. My physiological batteries were nearly dead. The room I was speaking in was shaped like a bowling alley except with a lower ceiling. And the sound system was the worst I'd worked with in months. The audience was staring at me, wondering what I would say to make listening worth their time.

What did I do?

Did I tell the audience that I was drained? Did I explain that my wife and five month old were both seriously ill with a bronchial infection and that I had not slept well the night before? Did I complain that the room set-up was untenable, that the audio engineer should be tortured and then executed, or that I had just done a splendid job for the audience that morning and they should have seen me then? Of course not. I rocked and rolled. I tapped deep into what hidden reservoir of energy I had left, drew upon every trick and technique I knew about presenting and gave the best presentation I was possible of giving and it was very well received.

Performance counts

Nobody knows how good you were before they encountered you and even fewer care. Whether you speak, do brain surgery, deliver the mail, manage an office or put out fires, the people who pay you depend on you to perform. They don't care how much you know and they may not even care how much you care. They care about how well you execute what you're expected to do.

Performance counts.

"I tried" are two of the most pathetic words an employer ever hears. You won't be rewarded for good intentions. The glory goes to those who achieve, not those who conceive. A good idea that isn't implemented is an exercise in intellectual futility. "Say what you'll do and do what you say" is the battle cry of the best. Don't make promises you can't keep.

Keep your promises in sync with your values, and then keep your promises.

The Problem with Vision

Business books and self-help writing have, in recent years, focused on the concept of vision, the ability to see a clear picture of a desirable future. It's importance is self-evident: it is easier to achieve that which is known. Vision is important, in part, because as Stephen Covey has popularized, one should begin with the end in mind.

I have coined the word "visioning." Vision is having a good idea; visioning is the ability to implement a good idea. Vision is about a concept; visioning is about activity. Having "vision" won't necessarily make you more successful or wealthier. Visioning will.

I have coined the word "visioning." Vision is having a good idea; visioning is the ability to implement a good idea. Vision is about a concept; visioning is about activity. Having "vision" won't necessarily make you more successful or wealthier. Visioning will.

The Problem with Being Really Smart

Many years ago I hired a college intern to do some marketing for my speaking business. Reese was a great guy and we soon became friends. One of the things that initially impressed me about Reese was his commitment to ongoing personal development. He read more books and listened to more self-help tapes than anybody I'd ever met.

Once, on coming back from a trip, I noticed a stack of books and several albums of tapes on Reese's desk. Given the inordinate amount of time he seemed to be studying and the depressing results he had been achieving, I felt it necessary to discuss the situation. "Reese, I've never said this to anyone before, but you study too much. You've got a head full of good ideas you've collected over the years from all your reading and listening. Now it's time to do something with that information. So quit studying and start doing!" I said. I learned from Reese that it is possible to substitute study for action. It is nothing more than procrastination in a pretty disguise. I would be the last to argue against ongoing learning. The problem occurs when it replaces consistent, persistent action.

Reese did go on to a highly successful career as a product manager with one of America's great computer companies. His success wasn't because of all he had learned. He succeeded by applying the information.

The Age of Wisdom

"The Information Age" has become a cliché. Originally coined as computers became a pervasive technology, the phrase misrepresents what is truly important about the age we live in.

Data is useless until it is organized. Organized data becomes information. Information is of no value until we understand it. Once understood correctly and consistently applied, information becomes knowledge. Knowledge does not benefit the holder until it is applied. When applied well, knowledge becomes wisdom. Wisdom is the correct and consistent application of knowledge.

Here's a good way to understand the difference between knowledge and wisdom. You know how to sign your name. On a scrap piece of paper, write out your full name. Have you done that? Good. Next, sign your name again directly underneath the first signature, but use your other hand. Unless you are ambidextrous, you'll immediately see a difference. Knowing how to sign your name is knowledge, but you typically do so correctly and consistently with only your dominant hand. I won't stretch the metaphor and say that your dominant hand possesses wisdom, but you get the point.

The best are known not for what they know, but for what they do. The Samurai maxim says, "To know and to act are one and the same." Wisdom enriches the quality of our lives, not just intellectually but pragmatically. Wisdom enables us to maximize experience. Therefore, the objective of learning is to leverage experience, past, present and future.

Wisdom is the correct and consistent application of knowledge.

The Winners Are Not Those Who Know; the Winners Are Those Who Do

There is a huge difference between what people are interested in and what they are actually committed to doing.

The Novotel New York, a hotel in midtown Manhattan, surveyed guests about their preferences. 71% of those surveyed said that gym facilities are important in deciding where they stay...but only 16% said they are likely to workout during their free time!

Why is execution so difficult for the average person or organization? This may well be one of the great mysteries of life. The best are known as those who say what they'll do and do what they say.

"Theory without practice is empty; practice without theory is blind."

– John Dewey

Once a useful idea is identified, the best look for ways to apply it to maximum advantage. They know that the speed with which the idea is implemented is nearly as important as the idea itself.

Once a useful idea is identified, the best look for ways to apply it to maximum advantage.

To Better Your Best, Improve Your IQ

By that, I don't mean "intelligence quotient." What matters even more is "implementation quotient." How can we increase our follow-through IQ?

First, consider the difference between an interest and a commitment. An interest suggests that you would enjoy or benefit from taking further action, but haven't actually decided to do so. A commitment is a decision to act.

I started speaking professionally when I was 18 and went full-time when I was 27. In my early years, it was tempting and easy to get distracted. For example, I regularly had audience members approach me after a speech or a seminar with "business opportunities." Most of those opportunities were multi-level marketing businesses, today called "network marketing." Network marketing has made many people very wealthy. The idea is that you recruit and enlist others into your "downline" or organization to both use and buy the products your company sells.

Here's why everyone wanted me in their business: as a speaker, I got to address and meet thousands of people each year. Wouldn't it be easy, they reasoned, to be a MegaVite (I'm making the name up) distributor and during or after every speech invite people to find out how they, too, could become rich as a MegaVite distributor?

Besides the obvious fact that my clients never paid me to promote MegaVite products, there was another reason I never pursued any network marketing opportunities. I have become convinced that becoming the best at anything in life is pretty much a full-time pursuit. I have devoted my primary professional energy into being the best speaker I am capable of being. MegaVite or any other network opportunity were for me a major distraction. While those side businesses might have been an interest, they were not a commitment.

If you really want to keep getting better at those areas in your life that are commitments, cut back on your interests. Identify the distractions that take away time and energy from your primary commitments.

Learn not to let those interests distract you. Tim Redmond captured this concept when he said, "There are many things that will catch my eye, but there are only a very few that catch my heart...it is those I consider to pursue."

Next, evaluate the reasonableness of your commitments. Have you made too many? Are they realistic in terms of your time, financial and skill resources? Trying to follow-through on too much results in accomplishing little. The only thing more draining than too many interests is too many commitments. That's where we get the phrase "spread too thin."

Track your commitments. Your follow-through on commitments needs to be 100%. From those commitments should flow an action plan. An action plan is different than a "to do" list. An action plan identifies those specific actions that need to be taken over time to completely implement an important idea or achieve closure on an important project. The best move from "the what" to "the how."

Once you've achieved a rational portfolio of commitments, both those major commitments you are pursuing as well as the little things you promise to do each day, the hardest but most important work becomes strategic execution.

Identify the distractions that take away time and energy from your primary commitments.

The Essentials of Strategic Execution

1. Use what you already know

"At the day of judgment we shall not be asked what we have read but what we have done."

- Thomas a Kempis

The critical question of execution is "where to begin?" The greater the value of an idea—whether for improvement or the accomplishment of a project—the more complex that idea is likely to be. Decisive action is often delayed because of the inability to identify a beginning point. The problem is not a lack of information. The problem is a lack of application.

Here's the homework. Do it now. Make a list of the best ideas for bettering your best that you already know. This includes ideas you've learned from this and other books, magazine articles, audio and video tapes and seminars you've attended. I challenge you to come up with at least three powerful ideas with which you are already familiar.

Write the best three ideas on an index card and put it in your daytimer, wallet or purse. Take it out at least twice a day. For the next week, use those ideas!! You already know them. It's time to benefit from them.

The greater the value of an idea, the more complex that idea is likely to be.

---

2. Look for leverage

Since truth is transferable, good ideas can often be creatively applied in several areas to affect improvement. I've learned the importance of leverage in writing. When I write an article, my objective is to get multiple uses from it. I can use key points in my speeches and seminars, publish it on my website, make it available to my corporate clients for their newsletters and internal communications, sell it to magazines for non-exclusive usage, record it in future audio or video training programs, make it available through my printed or electronic newsletters... You get the point.

Whenever you undertake a project or implement an idea, look for leverage. Ask, "How can I extend the use and benefits of this action?"

3. Practice the lost art of follow-through

The best follow a simple but powerful strategy: say what you'll do and do what you say. It's astounding how few people do that!

Consider: in the past two weeks, how many organizations or individuals have told you that they were going to do something...and then didn't do it? Consider also: what have you told others you'd do for them that never got done?

I don't know if follow-through was better or worse in the past. It doesn't really matter, because it seems abysmal today. The mark of a professional in any field is that they always deliver what they promise.

When they commit, it happens. I have a friend who is a successful entrepreneur who, prior to his retirement by age 40, ran a $75 million business. When we talk, whether its about business or personal matters, he makes a note of what he says he's going to do. And like clockwork, he follows through. I remark that I'd like to read an article that he mentioned, and it arrives in the mail two days later.

Follow-through is both a philosophy and a practice. Doing or not doing what we promise is a matter of integrity. Our reputations are not as good as our words, but our deeds. Inconsistency between what we say and do is lethal to integrity. The practice is straight forward. It requires a system of recording, dating and checking on commitments. One of the primary reasons why people don't follow-through is that they just forget. They wanted to make good on their promise, but it "slipped their mind." The cliché is valid: a short pencil is better than a long memory.

Inconsistency between what we say and do is lethal to integrity.

FOLLOW-THROUGH PLUS

Maybe the only thing better than doing what you promise is doing more than you promise. Since value-adding is always a priority, why not get creative and follow-through with a little more than you promised? In addition to my newsletter, I keep article reprints on file. When I promise to send someone my business card (I'd rather send it than just hand it to them because it makes more of an impact), I include a copy of my most recent newsletter or an article reprint along with the card.

And what about personal follow-through? How many commitments do you make to yourself that aren't kept?

4. Propel yourself with powerful reasons and passion

"Do every act of your life as if it were your last."

- Marcus Aurelius Antonius

You will accomplish much more in life if you have compelling reasons to execute boldly. Those reasons almost always come out of what you are passionate about. It is hard to execute a boring or mundane plan. We usually don't act dramatically on things that aren't dramatic to us.

Before you undertake an important course of action, ask yourself if you have compelling reasons to execute and follow-through. If you don't, your chances for failure are high.

5. Prepare prudently but not indefinitely

"Unless a decision has degenerated into work, it is not a decision; it is at best a good intention."

- Peter Drucker

Somewhere in between the paralysis of analysis and the rashness of action without preparation lies the best strategy: prepare prudently.

That means thinking through these basic questions:

1. Have I thought through the process of implementation?
2. Do I have compelling reasons to act?
3. Are these reasons consistent with my passion?

6. Get your team in place

One of the most common causes for failing to execute and implement is a breakdown in interdependence. Major projects require the input and cooperation of many people. Those who master the art of execution spend time identifying and gaining the support and commitment of those who will be necessary for the successful completion of the task—that's why relationship building is vitally important.

The best know that the more complex the challenge, the less likely that they possess all the resources and expertise necessary for completion. Total solutions require many smaller solutions, and those smaller solutions are usually possessed by many different people. Getting your team in place requires identifying all those players—colleagues, customers, vendors and others—who you will be interdependent with in completing the project

The objective of getting your team in place is to instill commitment.

Those who master the art of execution spend time identifying and gaining the support and commitment of those who will be necessary for the successful completion of the task.

---

7. Change your course but not your destination

Is this scenario familiar? An employer starts a major change initiative. Everybody starts—usually grudgingly—trekking off in a new direction. Suddenly management says, "Whoa! We've changed our minds...." and starts trying to round everybody back up. And in a surprisingly short period of time the initiative is dead in the water.

Execution often fails because we don't recognize the subtle difference between adjusting and abandoning our plans. Management starts a change initiative and sees it isn't working out as expected. Instead of adjusting the plan, they abandon it.

8. Aim for completion, not perfection

While good may be the enemy of best, perfection may well be the enemy of completion. How often do significant projects stall in the final stages because it became evident the outcome wasn't going to be perfect? Perfect is rarely the goal. Completion is more important than perfection, and here's why: once you complete a project, it is almost always easier to go back and polish the end result. But you can't polish or improve what you don't have.

A technique I use is called bombing. It is loosely adapted from the world of bodybuilding. Bodybuilders use very precise and specific routines to increase muscle mass. Doing a movement correctly is important not only for safety, but for achieving maximum effectiveness. There is another element that creates muscle growth, and that is intensity. Sometimes, at the end of a carefully orchestrated workout, a bodybuilder will bomb. They will take the focus off doing a movement perfectly and put the emphasis on doing it—any way they can. By temporarily throwing technique aside, they can stimulate maximally the muscle being worked.

To better your best, do whatever it takes to get it done. The objective is completion, not perfection. You can "bomb" a prototype by coming up with something that at least works. Afterwards, you can deal with style, dependability and price. It will be easier to improve a working prototype than to complete a perfect prototype on the first try.

Completion is more important than perfection.

---

9. Act on your implementation agenda

Recently, I was asked to develop a simple plan that the partners of an accounting firm could use for taking action after my presentation. I knew from experience that it was important for them to identify the best ideas they had received, and then develop a plan for implementing and benefiting from those ideas. I developed a worksheet that takes relatively little time to complete, but clearly details a plan for execution. Use it for ideas you find throughout this book, or for any meeting or conference you attend.

Execution Is Everything!

1. The important idea is ____________________

2. What I plan to do with this idea ______________

3. When I'll implement it ____________________

4. How I'll implement it (specifically what I'll do in terms of "action steps") ____________________
5. Who I plan to share this idea with ____________
6. What I'll ask them to do ____________________
7. When I'll ask them to have it completed ________
8. Benefit/consequence personally and organizationally

   ____

9. Follow-up timeline ____________________

Regrets, I've Had a Few

Cornell University researchers have discovered that life's biggest regrets almost always stem from what people don't do, as opposed to what they do. A study of 213 nursing home residents, retired professors, students and Cornell employees said it was a failure to act that haunted them rather than some specified action—by more than 2-to-1.

Tom Peters says fail forward faster. He believes it is through failure that we learn. I agree. Lots of mistakes are the hallmark of people who are trying lots of things. In the end, execution is everything.

Like the old adage says, "Sitting still and thinking makes no man great. The good Lord sends the fishes, but you must cast the bait."

11

The Continually Upgrading Organization

"I am captivated more by dreams of the future than by the history of the past."

– Thomas Jefferson

What keeps an organization, whether a corporation, a university, church or charity, from upgrading?

Many of the organizations I work with today have stopped dreaming. They are instead more preoccupied with the problems of the present than the hopes and aspirations of the future. They give lip service to improvement, but rarely know what that improvement looks like. They almost always have vision and mission statements, but these documents are embraced only by the consultants and executives who created them; employees rarely know or understand them, much less commit to them.

These are the organizations that change only when necessity and survival require it. And even then, they do so grudgingly. The interactions they have with employees, customers and vendors is economically motivated. The primary bond is money, not loyalty. As a result, they are organizations of interactions rather than relationships. As sterile as that arrangement seems, it works for these organizations. Because everyone involved understands the rules, no one is being cheated.

Formal communication is minimal. At these types of companies, employees still sometimes joke about mushroom management: bosses keep them in the dark and feed them manure. Most communication occurs informally; where there is a void, employees create information to fill it. Formal communication tends to move one direction: down. Chiefs tell bosses who tell supervisors who tell workers. Where there are suggestion boxes, the contents are smart-aleck remarks scribbled anonymously on index cards.

Learning is more often accidental than intentional. Training budgets are spent on videos, audios and books and the occasional one-day public seminar at a local hotel. There is rarely a team or organizational learning.

The strategy these companies take in the marketplace is "catch up" rather than "stay ahead." Pragmatism requires watching competitors. When they improve a product, lower a price or enhance a service, these organizations follow suit. Emulation rules the day.

These organizations are not socially irresponsible. They participate in the United Way Campaign, support the local youth sports leagues, etc. The investment is most often monetary. Little thought is given to a deep involvement, and there are no organizational causes save the odd revolutionary who keeps trying to rally the rest of the organization.

They are not dreamers, they are functionaries. Don't misunderstand what I'm saying: these organizations are not evil. They continue to produce results (for some reason, "grinding it out" is a phrase that comes to mind). They are not failures. They offer gainful employment to their people, they produce goods and services that are needed or at least desired, they continue to return enough to the bottom line that shareholders are placated and they have created a work environment that is comfortable if not enjoyable.

I speak of these organizations not with disdain, but with sadness. I am saddened by the reality described above because these organizations could achieve for themselves, their employees, their customers and their communities. They could be continually improving organizations, captured by the dream of a better future for all.

Complacency Kills

Several years ago a foreign government conducted a raid to rescue diplomats that had been held hostage for several months. Soldiers burst into the compound where diplomats were being held. Their surprise attack successfully rescued all but one hostage who was killed in the process. None of the terrorists survived. What were the terrorists doing at the time of the attack? Many of them were playing soccer.

There are more than a few companies today playing soccer with attacking forces outside their gates. Their success in fending off earlier sieges has created a deadly lethargy. They have been lulled into a false sense of security by their past successes. Their market position seems invincible. And management and employees have relaxed to enjoy their success.

I believe most individuals and companies that are successful for the long haul operate on a 50/50 mixture of fuel. They are powered by 50% heartfelt pride in the good work that they do and 50% gut-wrenching fear that, if they don't sustain extraordinary performance, they won't get to keep doing it. One counterbalances the other. With due vigilance, preparation and hard work, success can continue for prolonged periods.

Companies that are successful for the long haul operate on a 50/50 mixture of fuel.

Improving organizations don't get caught on the soccer field.

What Are the Ingredients for a Continuously Upgrading Organization?

Can infinite improvement be a template for organizations as well as for individuals? Can entire organizations not only commit to bettering their best, but implement processes for consistently doing so? I believe wholeheartedly that the answer to both questions is yes! I'll provide a picture, painting with wide brush strokes, of a perpetually improving organization.

Just what does a continually upgrading organization look like? It includes the following characteristics:

A Sense of Purpose

The pursuit of excellence is specific not generic. Whether an organization has a "mission statement," it must have a mission that gives point and purpose to all organizational efforts.

As an avid reader, I especially like the mission of Rodale Press: "Our mission is to show people how they can use the power of their bodies and minds to make their lives better. 'You can do it,' we say on every page of our magazines and books."

Serta's rallying motto? "We make the best mattress in the world."

Organizational mastery is also about responsibility. It has been said that citizens get the government they deserve. Likewise, I believe most of us work in the companies we deserve. I like to point out to clients that ultimately, "organizations" do nothing—only people do things.

The pursuit of excellence is specific, not generic.

A Predisposition to Change

"We got spoiled by our success," said the CFO of a large corporation, "For a while we said, 'We don't have competition.'" One of the most insidious enemies of improving organizations is complacency. Poor performers don't have the luxury of becoming complacent. They are usually scrambling to hang on. Companies that have become excellent, and have achieved market dominance, are candidates for a big fall. That's why in perpetually improving organizations, people who stir things up are highly prized. These are the people who rattle the cages, but they don't alienate people. They are skeptical, but not cynical. They are always questioning as a means of achieving continual improvement. If they were cynics, they would only criticize as spectators.

Improving organizations are, contrary to popular belief, not all that proactive. At least not in the literal sense.

You know that reactive is often the kiss of death for a company or association. Major change—in competition, regulation, technology—blindsides the unobservant. Sometimes even reacting quickly isn't enough.

So the popular opinion is to be "proactive."

You can be proactive at a micro level. You can institute a new ad campaign, redesign a product or whatever. But at a macro level—where the real impact of the world occurs—you are anything but proactive. Improving organizations are good at being interactive. They interact with the changes taking place in the world around them to create the outcomes they desire for their employees and their customers. They factor in trends, demographics, psychographics, currency exchange rates, commodity prices, regulations, social issues and a myriad of other factors, and from this cauldron of forces beyond their control, the leaders and employees of those organizations interact to create value and meaning.

Learning Individually and Collectively

Einstein said, "I have no special gift. I am only passionately curious." So, too, are improving organizations which learn better than the rest. They not only expect learning to take place, they require it.

Improving organizations focus their learning efforts to be inline with their mission and marketplace objectives. While they recognize that there is always value in employees having an enriched intellectual life, they focus on giving people opportunities to become better at the important work of the company.

Improving organizations focus their learning efforts to be inline with their mission and marketplace objectives.

The Strategic Use of Resources

Organizational stewardship is not about chanting "more with less" over and over. Improving organizations don't operate from a scarcity mentality. Stewardship is about the deployment of resources. At an individual level that means managing your time, expertise and the time and expertise of those on your team. At an organizational level, it means managing organizational resources with the same savvy and prudence as if they were your own.

Improving organizations want employees to think and act like owners. In addition to the philosophical rewards, it often means utilizing more substantive rewards. Improving organizations have programs like BYOB (build your own bonus). At most companies, there is a disincentive to using resources wisely. Department managers know at the end of the year any money left in their budget will probably be taken from them for the coming year.

BYOB rewards employees and managers for acting like stewards. At the end of the year, some percentage of whatever monies are left in the budget are distributed as a bonus to everyone in the department. The incentive becomes to make the most of resources and spend them carefully (departments are still held accountable for the measurable results that they are supposed to produce). If as a team you can save your department $100,000 and you know that 10% of that will come back to be distributed among team members, you have a solid reason to behave like a steward.

Improving organizations want employees to think and act like owners.

Execution

The three-letter extension that follows a period in PC file names indicates the type of information contained. For example, .exe, short for executable, means that double clicking on the file will launch a program or perform an operation. Many companies are files chock full of good ideas; the problem is that no .exe follows.

General George Patton said, "A good plan executed now is better than a perfect plan next week."

I have been espousing the same concept, only using different words. My take: the difference between excellence and mediocrity is the difference between common knowledge and consistent application.

The Japanese studied the U.S. electronics industry for many of the ideas that became platforms for very successful products. They didn't out-innovate us, but in some cases they out-implemented us. You don't have to be the most innovative if you can execute other people's ideas better.

Improving organizations decrease the distance between what they've learned and what they're doing with that information. There is individual accountability for results. One of the greatest barriers to execution in any organization is a lack of accountability that makes no one in particular responsible for results. It becomes too easy to blame other departments and individuals. Even if others have not fulfilled their roles, someone needs to be responsible. Part of accountability is being responsible for those who have committed to help achieve intended organizational results.

The difference between excellence and mediocrity is the difference between common knowledge and consistent application.

An Emphasis on Value-Creation

If value creation is paramount for individual and organizational success, why aren't employers teaching it? In more than 15 years working with companies, associations, non-profits, government agencies, schools and churches, I've yet to encounter an organization that has a course entitled, "How To Create Value" or "How To Make Yourself Valuable."

What people most need to learn isn't being taught! That's where I come in: I explain how to do it.

Does that mean that upgrading organizations don't teach value creation. Not necessarily. They may not have a course with that title, but somehow, some way, they must be diffusing practices throughout their firms that result in value creation. We know that the best continually create new value, so we know their employees must be contributing their talents. But very few if any organizations formally teach this critical skill.

What people most need to learn isn't being taught!

If you want your organization to be continually improving, teach grass-roots leadership and value-creation.

Rethink Everything

"If something has been done a particular way for fifteen or twenty years, it's a pretty good sign, in these changing times, that it is being done the wrong way."

- Elliot Estes

Improving organizations know it is dangerous to do business on "auto-pilot" (the way it's always been done.) They continually ask questions like these:

"What will most dramatically impact our business if we pursue and accomplish it?"

"What will give us the biggest payback on our investment of attention and capital?"

"How can we continually create new value for our customers?"

"How can we enrich the quality of work life for our employees?"

"How can we build mutually beneficial relationships with our vendors?"

Reinvention, at an organizational level, begins with basic questioning. It means looking at every aspect of your business, and then asking these three questions:

Should we be doing it?

If not, what should we be doing instead?

Improving organizations frequently play "what if?" How can we do it more, better, faster, less, "funner," different?

The answers to these questions, however, are not made in a vacuum. Improving organizations never do anything without considering the impact on it's important constituents. Those constituents include:

- customers
- vendors
- shareholders
- colleagues
- community

The million dollar question then becomes: Will they value the change(s)?

Constant and Compelling Communication

"The objective is to have all 4,500 people know what matters. If people don't have total access to information, they have to guess at what they should be doing."

– Dave Duffield, CEO of PeopleSoft Inc.

In upgrading organizations, information is freely available to all. The premise is simple: if employees are expected to act responsibly like owners, they must have access to the kind of information owners have to make decisions.

These organizations clarify expectations and responsibilities. Dr. Eugene Jennings at Michigan State University studies performance problems in the workplace and found that 43% were directly traceable to the fact that employees didn't know what they were supposed to do.

But simply making information available and clarifying expectations are only a small part of how improving organizations communicate. Most importantly, they pursue truth telling. Improving organizations have no tolerance for foolishness or stupidity, regardless of where it resides in the organization. That's why truth telling is so important.

I am often amazed that well-meaning managers can create or at least sustain such incredible levels of dysfunction and incompetence. Bring a group of top management together, and as a group they seem very sane. Seldom can you identify the dissenter or dissenters. To the observing eye, most management teams seem dedicated and sincere.

Someone knows who the idiots are: the people who work with them. Group denial isn't quite what's going on. It's more like group rationalization. The exception occurs in continually improving organizations. They have zero tolerance for this kind of person. When the problem becomes apparent, it is dealt with. Not by employees. They have no formal authority in reprimanding or removing the problem individual. Leadership stomps down hard. The message is change or leave. Effective leadership roots out stupidity, whether it lies in people or policies.

It might mean a regular "search and destroy" mission conducted by managers to identify those things that keep employees from doing better. More often it is an ongoing awareness—an ear to the ground—to find out where or who the problems are.

In upgrading organizations, information is freely available to all.

For some of you reading this book, the greatest barrier to your organization's improvement is an individual or cadre of similar individuals that leadership has never had the gonads to deal with. If you're leadership, this is a wake up call for you. If you're an employee, and it becomes apparent management is going to allow this to continue, this may be a wake-up call for you—to start an active job search for an organization with zero tolerance for stupidity, either in it's people or it's practices.

Customers Have Relationships with People, Not Companies

"Treat people as though they were what they ought to be and you help them become what they are capable of being."

- Goethe

When improving organizations communicate, they tell the truth. They are blatantly honest, but that doesn't mean they are brutally frank. They know that a primary objective of relationship building is to maintain and improve relationships, not end them unless absolutely necessary.

Improving organizations build-up rather than diminish those who work there. They know, like Goethe suggested, that what you expect from people in large part determines what you get from them. Therefore, they have high expectations of coworkers. The organization runs a fast race with leaders at the front of the pack. Leadership expects much because leadership sets the standard by their own performance and behavior.

When improving organizations communicate, they tell the truth.

At Disney, they say that street sweepers are the most important cast members. There is a pragmatism to this. In addition to keeping their parks spotlessly clean, street sweepers are readily accessible to guests who have questions. Much of the Disney experience is created by those front-line cast members. Because Disney treats street sweepers as significant, they do significant work. Herein is a secret of improving organizations: if you want no insignificant employees, treat everyone as significant.

Which would you choose: to be a team leader or be on a team of leaders? Neither is without significant responsibility, but each is starkly different than the other. The Leader is a visionary or charismatic individual who sets the course of direction for a team. John Maxwell says, "Vision is the gift of the leader to the followers. Fulfillment of the vision is the gift of the followers to the leader." An important thought, eloquently worded, and yet still the reference is to "the leader."

Would a team or business prosper if they were populated not by a single leader and many followers, but "many leaders"? Do too many cooks spoil the broth, or, as Stan Davis found when researching his book Blur, do many cooks actually improve the broth? For most groups, there will always be The Leader. But my observation is that the best organizations are those with leadership developed throughout.

What percentage of each day does the designated leader of your group spend in contact with colleagues and customers? Or, what percentage of customers and colleagues have regular, relationship-enriching contact with him or her? For both questions, the answer is usually "extremely small." Leaders do interact regularly with other leaders and key customers. The primary interface between employees and customers, however, does not occur at high leadership levels. Even leaders who consciously attempt to increase contact with employees and customers are limited by their available time.

The best organizations are those with leadership developed throughout.

What would happen if, whenever team members interacted with each other or customers, each took a personal responsibility to lead? The quality of each interaction, and the resulting quality of products or services delivered, would soar.

The best employers don't demand "human sacrifices;" they don't expect managers and employees to give up their families, health or self-esteem in the pursuit of corporate goals and objectives. They recognize that many have strip-mined the talent and enthusiasm of their workers, so upgrading organizations treat employees as the renewable resource.

"You teach what you know, but you reproduce what you are."

– John Maxwell

To be an improving organization, you need fewer managers and more mentors. Improving organizations must have leaders who invest themselves in stretching, growing and developing others. I often ask clients if they would like to add employees without increasing their payroll and the answer is always a resounding yes. What if you were able to help 10 employees grow by 10% in the next 12 months? That means you would have created the equivalent of another unit of contribution, as you have 10 people accomplishing the work of 11. 10% x 10 Employees x 12 Months = 11 Employees. More contribution, same payroll.

The problem with layoffs and downsizing is that in many cases they are a short-term solution to a long-term problem. The alternative to reducing head count is releasing and developing the talent that is already in your employ. Improving organizations have a disproportionate number of coaches within their ranks. These "coaches" (or counselors or mentors or whatever you choose to call them) know that employees grow when they have a relationship with others who possess these skills:

They are interested in you, you aren't just a means to an end.

They notice what you do right, as well as what you do wrong.

They give you suggestions on how to improve.

They don't just instruct, they inspire.

They show you how what you do helps or hurts the team.

They're honest, even when it isn't easy.

As a result, employees grow and improve, and that drives the improvement of the organization.

The alternative to reducing head count is releasing and developing the talent that is already in your employ.

A Larger Purpose

One of Zig Ziglar's most often quoted principles is this: if you help enough people get what they want and need, they'll help you get what you want and need. Upgrading organizations attract and keep top-notch individuals by providing the things most important to them. These needs include but are not limited to:

Pay proportionate to performance.

Continual learning to increase employability.

The chance to make both money and meaning.

Shared reward for shared sacrifice.

Challenge, not convenience.

Leadership worth following.

The opportunity to create rather than just replicate.

Great organizations pay well. It is foolish to think that you can attract and keep superior talent with average compensation. If you want better employees, then pay better wages and salaries. But pay isn't enough. Competitive pay is what it takes to get into the game. Improving organizations do more than provide an opportunity for people to make money. They respond to the contemporary challenge of enabling employees to make money and meaning.

> **"They don't want to work for a company, they want to work for a movement, something that has a larger meaning and gives them a sense of purpose about what they are doing."**
>
> **- Yvon Chouinard**

Meaning can be derived from a number of interactions, but key areas are relationships and service. Employees want to feel proud of where they work and who they work for (that's why character is an important issue for leadership). They want to be part of a winning team (that's why marketplace success is about more than profit). They want to enjoy who they work with. Work relationships can consume as much or more of our days as do our personal relationships.

But even those things aren't enough. Employees at improving organizations have an opportunity to leave a legacy beyond themselves or their organizations. This is the age of volunteerism. Being of service to others in the community prevents the self-absorption that is prevalent in many organizations today. Being successful enough to share the wealth of that success with others gives a larger purpose to corporate performance. People feel they've been paid for their efforts, but receive an equal or greater reward by being of service to others outside their organizations walls.

The improving organization knows it has a responsibility to the community. As the organization improves, so should the community, and that occurs through service.

Beyond Jobs

Jobs aren't big enough for people. No matter how enlightened, concerned and caring any organization becomes, the great insight of the new millennium for employers should be that jobs alone can't define us. Like a plant fed only one of several needed nutrients, an employee consumed by their work becomes stunted. The resulting organism bears little resemble to the healthy one.

Which brings us full circle to the point of upgrading. These skills can indeed be used individually and collectively, but not exclusively for the pursuit of organizational success or profit. If the people within an organization aren't growing—if they aren't receiving all the nutrients necessary to sustain life—then the organization will eventually suffer, even as it tries to cycle through new employees to replace those who have lost their passion and commitment for work.

Jobs aren't big enough for people. No matter how enlightened, concerned and caring any organization becomes, the great insight of the new millennium for employers should be that jobs alone can't define us.

The Mystery of Leadership

There is no recipe. Not for an improving organization. There are guidelines and principles, like those I've outlined. There are role models and examples. But no recipes.

Instead, there is mystery. Managers prefer recipes, templates and designs guaranteed to work every time. Leaders know there are no such things. They willingly enter into the mystery of leadership and development. They take the best practices and ideas they glean from others—colleagues, customers, vendors, authors, consultants, friends and family—and throw them into their tool kit. Then they undertake the hard but rewarding work of finding what will work for them, and for their organization. Over time—using science and art, trial and error—they create something always valuable and rare: an improving organization that continuously upgrades.

Managers prefer recipes, templates and designs guaranteed to work every time. Leaders know there are no such things.

12

How to Upgrade Every Day

"It is never too late to be what you might have been."

– George Elliot

The Squirrel Proof Bird Feeder

My friend Bill is a successful speaker and author. For relaxation, he likes to watch birds. Several years ago he bought a new house on the edge of a wooded area. The first weekend he lived there, he put a bird feeder up in his back yard. Before the sun set that night, squirrels were swinging off the bird feeder, eating the feed and scaring the birds away. For the next two weeks, Bill tried everything short of violence to keep the squirrels out of his bird feeder. Nothing worked.

In desperation, he visited the local hardware store. There he found an unusual looking bird feeder with wire mesh wrapped around it. It was called, enticingly, the Squirrel Proof Bird Feeder. And it was guaranteed. He purchased it and put it up in his back yard. Before the end of that day, the squirrels were swinging off the Squirrel Proof Bird Feeder and still scaring the birds away.

Now Bill was frustrated. He took the feeder down and returned to the store where he'd bought it. He was a little worked up by now and demanded a refund. The store manager responded, "Calm down. I'll give you a refund, but you need to understand: there is no such thing as a squirrel proof bird feeder." Now Bill was curious. "You mean to tell me that we can put people into space on a regular basis. We can communicate in a matter of seconds anywhere on the planet. But our best scientists and engineers can't figure out how to design and manufacture a bird feeder that will keep out a rodent with the brain the size of a pea. Is that what you're trying to tell me?" Bill asked.

"Yeah," said the store manager, "I'm just not taking as much time to tell you." Even more curious, Bill asked for an explanation.

The store manager said, "Sir, to explain it, I need to ask you two questions. First, how much time have you spent on average each day trying to keep the squirrels out of your bird feeder?" Bill thought about it for a bit and replied, "I 'dunno. Probably 10 or 15 minutes a day."

"That's what I thought," said the manager. "Now, second question. How much time do you think the squirrels spent each day trying to get in?"

Intuitively, Bill knew the answer: every waking squirrel moment.

I was so intrigued by the story, that I did some additional study on squirrels. Squirrels spend 98% of their waking time foraging for food. Focused attention beats brains and brawn every time!

Upgrading doesn't necessarily require another degree or a bigger computer. What it does require is the ability to focus your time and expertise. And if you focus better than your competition, you'll surpass them.

Upgrading is the ability to focus your time and expertise.

The 3 Most Important Resources of Success

How often have you heard "Time is money?" It isn't true: time isn't money—its worth much, much more. You can enjoy time without money. But you can't enjoy money without time.

When I ask people to identify their most limited resources, money usually heads the list. Money isn't really a resource. We are not born into the world with it, entitled to it or guaranteed of keeping it once we get it. It is a unit of exchange, a byproduct of how we invest our true resources. The three most important resources within your control are:

- your time
- your expertise
- the time and expertise of others

How you invest those three resources ultimately determines the value you create and the resultant wealth you enjoy.

The problem, as Irene Peter observed, "Life is entirely too time-consuming." Twenty years ago futurists predicted we'd be working only 20 hours a week. Today the average American works 48 hours each week. The problem isn't how busy we are, but rather how we are busy. The problem for many today is that they aren't investing their time to better themselves, their relationships or their organizations. They are squandering the essence of their lives being entertained, rather than educated or enlightened.

According to John Robinson and Geoffrey Godbey, authors of Time for Life, adults average 39.4 hours of free time each week, up from 34.8 in 1965. They use 15 hours watching TV! They spend 6.7 hours socializing, 4.4 hours communicating via phone, mail and conversations, 2.8 hours reading, 2.2 hours involved in education, 2.2 hours engaging in recreation and sports, 1.2 hours in groups, .9 hours in cultural events, .9 hours involved with religion, and .4 hours with radio/recordings. To understand your current level of success, consider changing how you spend your time.

Stewardship

At a young age I learned the concept of stewardship—a wise use of the resources that we have been given. Good stewards know that their most valuable resources—life itself and the natural resources of the world around them—are gifts. They were born into the world with these gifts and have a responsibility to their creator to use them wisely.

You determine how to spend your time each day. Consider: the wealthiest and most successful people in the world have the same number of seconds, minutes and hours in their day as you, no more, or no less. The difference is whether you spend your time, or invest it wisely. To better your best, become a skilled steward of these resources. The following will explain how to develop these critical skills.

The wealthiest and most successful people in the world have the same number of seconds, minutes and hours in their day as you, no more, or no less.

MVP Activities

The ability to prioritize and focus on doing the most important things is a defining characteristic of the best.

In sport, MVP stands for "most valuable player." I suggest you revise the acronym to stand for "most valuable and profitable." The key to stewardship is to focus on your MVP activities: those that give you the biggest payback on your investment of time and expertise.

What 8-10 activities, if you spent 60-80% of every day doing them, would provide you with the greatest achievement and satisfaction in your career or business? Make a Top 10 MVP Activity list. Think about all the different things you do each day in your work. The average person engages in more than 150 different activities each day. Then identify your top 10 MVP activities and commit to spending 60-80% of every day doing them. That still leaves you with 20-40% of each day to deal with emergencies, interruptions and other imposed distractions.

Ideal Day

The reason why most people don't enjoy more "ideal days" is that they don't know what an ideal day is. My colleague Thom Winninger challenged me with this concept. He suggested I write down those activities that made an ideal day for me. I took two weeks. I started my list on my laptop computer. I brainstormed, shrank the list and synthesized. I finally came up with eight activities that I consider constitute an ideal day.

I don't want to confuse you at this point. Not everything on my ideal day list is an MVP activity. MVP activities produce results. Ideal Day activities may or may not be the same thing. One of the items on my ideal day list was: Unrushed, enjoyable and healthy meals. I had found that many of my meals were grabbed on the run, and they often included fast food that wasn't that good for me. In an ideal day, that wouldn't happen.

Thanks to Thom's suggestion, I now have a template for an ideal day. Not only do I know what an ideal day looks like, I can now schedule and plan for those things that make for an ideal day!

The reason why most people don't enjoy more "ideal days" is that they don't know what an ideal day is.

The Big Trick

I've found that you can create more ideal days using one simple and powerful technique: to make good on a personal commitment (exercise, more sales calls, more family time, whatever) you have to make the commitment essential.

I completed an interesting experiment during the first quarter of 1994. I was traveling nearly non-stop giving speeches and seminars. Sandwiched between engagements was a three day period of time to be spent in the studio recording a new video series on mastering change. Professionally, things couldn't have been any busier.

I had always regretted that during these periods, I would often go several days without any exercise. Travel had always disrupted my workouts, whether in the gym or on the running track. The reason, of course, was that although I fancied myself committed to exercise, I usually treated it as expedient: I did it when I could.

At the time I made my list, I was scheduled to work 40 days in a row. This test wasn't about life balance. Here's what had happened. I was working on a new video about managing change. That involved pre-production, production and post-production work that was scheduled in the midst of a very busy speaking schedule. I was either working on the video, flying to or from a speech or giving a speech.

I figured if I could exercise every day during one of the busiest periods of my life, then I'd know I could exercise every day. The test was to see if it was possible. My primary commitment was to fulfilling my responsibilities to clients and others. Then I decided, I would do whatever it took to get some form of exercise. Some days I was able to spend an hour in a gym. Other days I exercised in my hotel room. One day I was so tired I stopped in the middle of a run in a city park and took a nap. I made a breakthrough: I did it! I got some exercise every day of that crazy period. When I reflected on how I accomplished it, I discovered the big trick.

Most things in our lives we do each day because they are expedient; we "get around to them." Expedient is good for interests; essential is necessary for commitments. Here's the big trick: move your ideal day activities from "expedient" to "essential." Expedient activities are those you do if you can: if it is easy, quick or convenient. Essential activities are those you make happen, even if they aren't expedient.

Make your ideal day list essential rather than expedient and you'll find yourself enjoying more ideal days.

Entropy

In physics, the law of entropy says that all systems, left unattended, will run down. Everything tends towards disorganization. Watches don't build, wind or repair themselves. Without an outside influence, like the electricity from a battery or the skills of a jeweler, the watch wears out over time. The best know that entropy is an enemy of greatness.

If you suddenly stopped doing those things that made you successful, chances are someone would notice and alert you. Your boss would be quick to tell you if you weren't doing those things she expected. Your customers would point out that you aren't delivering the value they've come to depend on. Your spouse would let you know that the relationship was suffering because you no longer brushed your teeth.

The bigger danger is that you will start doing those things that made you successful a little less. You won't cease the behaviors that made you a success, you'll simply devote less time and attention to them. The demise is so gradual that is it almost imperceptible. Nobody, including you, notices until it is too late.

The best know that entropy is an enemy of greatness.

Don't let entropy ruin your stewardship. To better your best, periodically ask yourself this question: What did I do in the past that made me successful that I'm not doing as much or as well in the present? Why not approach your life as a series of moments rather than going for "the big hit," that event or activity that is so powerful that it changes you forever? Try living each moment as an opportunity to upgrade. Upgrade the moments and you've upgraded your entire life. Here's how:

1. Show up all the time

We need to manage the present moment.

The best do plan carefully, and they reflect on the past to draw lessons and insights from it. They do a better job of managing the present moment than the rest. They live fully in the here and now, neither day-dreaming, bemoaning the past nor fretting about the future.

2. Pace yourself

When I was younger, I was an expert at burning the candle at both ends. My motto was "I'll sleep when I'm dead." As I aged, I realized I was going to be dead a lot sooner if I didn't start sleeping more! You can't run on full-speed without burning up your metabolic engine. The negative affects of stress are often caused by an excess of adrenaline. If you stay pumped on adrenaline all the time, you'll impair your ability to perform and live life fully.

"The daily plan" is probably one of the most preached and practiced time management techniques in history. But does it really work? For many, the idea of making a list of things to do each day doesn't work as well as it could because it doesn't factor in the concept of pacing. To take advantage of pacing requires that the daily plan be part of a weekly plan, and both plans need to be committed to writing. Even the best memories fail at consistently tracking important tasks and projects.

Why a weekly plan? Let's say that you have 43 things to do next week, ranging from the somewhat minor to the really major. When do you plan to do them? First thing Monday morning you'll make a list of all 43 to do that day. You don't really expect to get them all done on Monday, but you figure you'll accomplish the lion's share.

When the dust has settled at the end of the day, your list is now up to 47. Not only have you not accomplished most of what you tried to do, but some things have come up that you've had to add to your list. Tuesday morning you start, full speed, to accomplish the list that had grown to 47 on Monday.

And by noon on Tuesday, you're so frustrated by how many items are still on the list that you wad it up and throw it out the window.

Planning one week at a time gives a greater sense of control by taking advantage of the concept of pacing. It allows us to focus, not on a single day, but on a longer period of time that's more manageable. An important key to getting more done is having both a daily and weekly plan that allows you to distribute your activities and workload rationally.

3. Prioritize

Have you noticed that if you have a list of things to do today, and by the end of the day if you've accomplished all but one, the one thing you have yet to do is the most important item on the list? That's because of "reverse prioritization." Here's how it happens. The easy things can be done quickly, and by checking off a lot of them, we feel a sense of accomplishment. We, of course, keep putting off the biggest and most difficult tasks until we're out of time.

That's why you need to prioritize every item on your daily plan. As famed author Stephen Covey says, you need to do first things first.

Ever heard that good is enemy of best? The problem for most of us isn't in choosing between good and bad; but between good, better and best. Priorities, like an intimate understanding of your top 10 MVP activity list, keep us focused on what's best.

4. To optimize, systemitize

The system you use is less important than the fact that you use a single system and that you use it consistently.

I'm sure there are some fine selling points for each and every time management system on the market today, but I recommend that you carefully select a system you're willing to commit to for at least the next year.

When choosing your system, remember these things. First, price is not an accurate predictor of usefulness. Put substance above style when choosing your system. Secondly, keep it as simple as possible. The system should free up time for you, not consume it. Thirdly, don't get too technical. My basic time management system goes in a ringed binder and is full of pencil marks and erasures. If you have to log onto your computer to use your time management system, you may not use it as much as you should.

The system you use is less important than the fact that you use a single system and that you use it consistently.

---

5. Take charge of your time

Although we can't control everything that occurs each day, most people can control much more than they are. Many of us become victims of other people who, lacking the system and the skills, create crises that impact us. But there are things we can do to manage our interactions with others, even those who don't plan.

When Jeff Salzman, co-founder of CareerTrack, first met Scott Peck, best selling author of "The Road Less Traveled," he was surprised to learn that Peck spends one hour each day doing nothing but thinking. And yet Peck is a prolific writer and speaker. It is fascinating that truly productive people aren't always as busy as we think they might be.

6. Dump perfectionism

> **"True workaholics are defined as people who are addicted to the process of working, irrespective of the results of their labor. "**
>
> **-Anonymous**

I used to be a card carrying perfectionist, proud that I had extremely high standards. But I didn't realize that there was a difference between having the high standards of excellence and being a perfectionist. A clinical psychologist once defined a perfectionist as someone who has a neurotic attention to details, usually stemming from insecurity. For a perfectionist, nothing is ever good enough; not because they are committed to success, but because they are afraid of inadequacy.

Excellence is something entirely different. Excellence is a commitment to high standards that means additional time or energy invested to a task or product makes it noticeably better to the end-user. Time or energy that doesn't create value is wasted.

Thomas Edison said, "I don't want to invent anything that nobody wants to buy." I never want to be guilty of spending time on a project, product or a service if it doesn't create value to the end user. We need to involve the customer in defining quality, whether that customer is a coworker, our boss, or an employee. Sometimes our definition of "value" doesn't match the definition of those we serve. That's why the end-user helps define true value.

When I was growing up, my parents used to say that everything worth doing is worth doing well, but Mom and Dad were telling me a half-truth. Some things are worth doing and getting done. Some things are worth doing well. And other things are worth doing very, very well. Perfectionism is the inability to know the difference.

7. Develop discipline

Discipline is doing what needs to be done. It is the ability to delay immediate gratification in order to obtain long-term gratification. We often know what needs to be done. And it's not that we lack the ability to do it. It's that we lack the discipline to do it. Will Rogers said, "Plans will get you into things but you have got to work your way out."

Sometimes discipline can be accomplished by removing temptation. (The near-impossible-to-resist urge for channel surfing by men is a prime example.) What time-wasters in your life could you eliminate? Are there temptations you need to remove?

Discipline is the ability to delay immediate gratification in order to obtain long-term gratification.

---

8. Convert dead-time to head-time

The average person spends 30 minutes each day waiting and that figure doesn't include time commuting in your car. I recommend that you convert "downtime" to "development time." Carry a small note pad so you can jot down ideas. Keep a good book, magazine or other reading material in your briefcase. And, as previously mentioned, don't forget to keep educational audio cassettes in your car so you can learn while you drive. Discipline yourself to make the most of downtime.

9. Leverage yourself

Nobody can do it all by herself.

Even if you don't formally manage people, your success in life is predicated on how well you get along with others. The only way you'll gain their cooperation is through your ability to create enjoyable and rewarding relationships. We need to be able to get commitment from others to help us achieve what we desire. Trying to do it all yourself will severely limit how much you can accomplish. In leveraging yourself, you can fine-tune your interactions with others.

At the next performance appraisal, have your staff or employees come prepared to answer these three questions about your performance as a manager.

Question #1: "What am I doing that helps and supports you the most?" Begin on a positive note by identifying the supportive behaviors that you should keep doing or do more of in your interactions with the employee.

Question #2: "What would you like me to consider not doing or doing differently?" Notice that the important word I used is "consider". A reverse performance appraisal doesn't necessarily mean that I'll do whatever an employee requests. It simply says that I take them seriously enough to consider their feedback and that, based on that feedback, I will either do as they suggest, or at the very least, explain why I'm not.

Question #3: "What would you like me to consider doing that I'm not currently doing?" Very often, there are several things that we could do to support an employee that we aren't aware of because we don't know how that particular coworker wants to be treated.

10. Do it now!

Procrastination kills improvement, so the best spend less time preparing and much time doing.

Two techniques of dealing with change also apply in managing your scarce resource of time. First: identify the first step first. Procrastination is often a result of having so much to do that we don't do anything. Disregard the additional steps and effort that will be required for completion. Once you've begun, you've triumphed over procrastination.

The second technique is to divide activities up into bite-sized pieces. Find a piece of the project that can be completed during whatever period of time is available. Over the course of a week or two, you've completed what you once put off doing. And you've done it one bite at a time.

11. Fear neither failure nor success

The fear of failing prevents many people from ever trying.

Clearly defined, failure is a means of learning and growth. It's even okay to make the same mistake as long as you're trying something new. However, there should be a reasonable limit to how many mistakes you could make before the cost of the lesson becomes too high. If you make the same mistake three times, you're obviously not learning from past experience.

The author Elbert Hubbard said, "To avoid criticism, do nothing, say nothing, be nothing."

I have observed that the people who win big are those who were also willing to fail big. Try and you may not succeed, but never try and you'll never succeed.

Psychologists have found that as crippling as a fear of failure might be, so is a fear of success. Some people fear the increased expectations that they have to live up to when they're successful, so they sometimes short-circuit themselves in their attempts to improve. The tough thing about being successful is that people expect you to keep being successful. Again, the wisdom of the ages is true: it is better to be a has-been than a never-was. A fear of failure or a fear of success can be a very real barrier in your attempt to get things done. Accept that failure and success are not mutually exclusive.

Try and you may not succeed, but never try and you'll never succeed.

---

12. Don't spend or save time, invest it

When I was in college, I had a roommate who had a sign above his desk that read "What is the best use of my time right now?"

Sometimes goofing off is a pretty good use of time.

For example, maybe you need a break for a few minutes to recharge your batteries. The problem is, a lot of us are living our lives on auto pilot. We are not consciously choosing how to spend each moment of each day. I'm not suggesting that we should become robots, that we should become so driven that we don't have a free moment or a leisure moment in the course of a day. But we need to consciously choose how to best utilize our time.

Lou Holtz, formerly the head coach of the fighting Irish of Notre Dame popularized the acronym WIN which stands for What's Important Now? If we are able to identify the best use of our time—what's important now—we'll find our time invested rather than simply spent.

What is the best use of my time right now?

Make Every Day Your Best

I've developed a check list for a successful day and I'd like to share it with you.

Did I tell or show someone that I loved them?

Did I compliment or praise someone I live or work with today?

Did I read a book or listen to a tape that stimulated my thinking?

Did I increase my skill in my profession?

Did I do something for good health?

Am I closer to my goals than when I woke up this morning?

Did I do anything tough or challenging to build discipline?

Did I do something just for the pure joy of it?

Have I taken time to reflect on the lessons of the day?

Have I planned for another successful day tomorrow?

If you can answer yes to most of these questions, you have been a truly masterful steward of the day.

What's the Best Use of Your Time—Right Now?

Upgrading isn't only about investing your time, energy and expertise to create monetary wealth. It is about bettering your best in all areas of your life, and in the process increasing the greater wealth of living.

As I've aged, and hopefully matured in the process, I've come to redefine "productivity." I want the things I do each day to not simply create results, but to enrich the quality of my life. I've got to be honest: on most days, I love my life. God has been gracious. There are times of sadness, pain and struggle, but they pale in comparison to the good things I enjoy. And I need to continually remind myself of that so that I don't lose perspective.

It is easy to get caught up in the process of doing versus accomplishing. I have begun to ask myself that question more often. Not, "What am I doing?" but "What am I accomplishing?"

Execution—implementing boldly—should be about accomplishment, not activity.

We all feel the frustration of juggling "multiple lives." I am a business owner, manager, professional speaker, author, husband, father, son, brother, friend, lay person and organization leader. Our roles are acted out against a changing backdrop. It is easy to get caught up in the "doing trap" only to miss accomplishing what is really important. Here's an example:

Long weekends tend to create a certain amount of pressure on the first day back to work. A few short years ago we had just celebrated the Memorial Day weekend and I wanted to hit it hard the next day. I was in the gym at 5:30 a.m., fed my 9 month old son Hunter at 6:45 a.m. and was ready to leave the house at 7:15 a.m. Somehow, Hunter always figured out when I was leaving. He got upset, scrunched up his face and started to cry. There were few things in life that broke my heart like that did.

On my first attempt to leave, Hunter won me over. I took him from Darla and started to walk him around the house. He was at the tottering phase—ready to walk but unable to do so unassisted. He wanted to go into the master bathroom and went immediately to the full length mirror. Babies love to look at themselves in the mirror. I'm not sure, but I think they think there is an identical baby staring back at them. Darla and I sat on the floor and laughed as Hunter had a big time playing in the mirror.

And I realized that it didn't matter if I got to the office 15 minutes or an hour later than I had planned. As it turned out, I did accomplish a great deal that day, but nothing occurred at the office that was memorable. Hunter taking those tentative steps along the mirror was memorable. I'm glad I didn't make the poor exchange of a few extra minutes of work time for a timeless memory of my son. Soon he'll be grown and as busy as his Dad. My only hope is that somehow, in these early years, he'll somehow remember that he had a father that made the time to spend with him instead of always rushing off to the office or the airport. Yes, I do travel much and work hard. But I've learned, and not too late, about the importance of making meaning over the drive to make money.

Execution—implementing boldly—should be about accomplishment, not activity.

13

Conclusions

"As I grow to understand life less and less, I learn to live it more and more."

- Jules Renard

The longer I live, the more mysterious life becomes to me. The older I get, the more I enjoy my life. There are some physical disadvantages, but the psychological advantages far outweigh them. Shortly before his death, my beloved colleague Cavett Robert often told me that at his age, well into his eighties, "Food tastes better and music sounds sweeter...."

I've devoted much of my career and this entire book to the subject of improvement. I tackled an even more daunting subject, really, and that is once you become the best at what you do, how do you keep getting better? My study in numerous fields ranging from economics to theology has led me to the conclusion that improvement is infinite. No matter how good we become, we can still get better. And I see that not as obligation, but opportunity.

B.C. Forbes, himself a fantastically successful businessman, once said, "Let us never forget that the business of life is living, not business." I'd like to overlay where we've been in the preceding chapters with four final challenges that I hope will bring you happiness and enjoyment as much as they bring you improvement and success.

Let us never forget that the business of life is living, not business.

---

1. Choose carefully how you organize your life

Organizing principles are those elements we use, consciously and often unconsciously, to structure our lives. Some choose those principles and live life by design. Others adopt these principles unaware and end up living life by default.

For most people, there are four ways to organize one's life. You can center your efforts on

- Rewards
- Results
- Recreation
- Relationships

Those who focus on rewards place a priority on what they personally enjoy. Hedonism as a school of philosophy was about satisfying the senses as fully as possible. The focus was the pursuit of pleasure. Hedonism has a major philosophical flaw: the more pleasure your pursue and enjoy, the more you want. Our desire for pleasure is insatiable. If you make eating a priority, it is a short distance from gourmand to glutton.

In the age of consumerism we work not for the pleasure of the job but for the rewards the work makes possible. This exchange of effort for things isn't entirely bad. But as a practical point, ask those you know who have the most "stuff" if their stuff has truly made them happy. You might be surprised at what they tell you.

The second organizing principle is results. People who value results above all else are usually very competent and effective human beings. Their enjoyment comes from what they accomplish, regardless of the tangible rewards. "A job well done" makes them happy, not because they can buy a more powerful snow blower, but because of the recognition of the results they produced.

Again, there is nothing inherently good or bad about organizing your life around results. But like hedonism, how do you know when you're results are enough? Is there an objective measure that says your record of results has put you at the top of the heap? That you are the number one results-producing individual in your field? In the history of the world? Of course not.

The third way to organize your life is around recreations. Make the pursuit of adventure and excitement your principal aim. Work enough to be able to spend your evening and weekends at the lake or riding your motorcycle or boardsailing. Unfortunately, I've found that the more toys I have in my garage, the less time I have to enjoy them. I love recreation and I've pursued adventure all over the world. But as an end objective, I've found it lacking.

The fourth organizing principle is relationships. The focus here is on the quality of the interactions with others and the bonds formed. We often call individuals with this organizing principle "people persons." They value relationships above results or rewards. Their pleasure is derived from the quality of the relationships they have with family, friends, colleagues and customers.

Is there a downside to organizing around relationships? There can be. The stereotypical "good old boy" or "good old gal" seems content to get along rather than contribute in society. They are well-liked, but not known for being productive or financially successful.

I have observed and do know people who are dominant in one of these four organizing principles. Most of us, however, have learned to be successful in life by combining organizing principles, or even doing a change-up when it served our purposes.

The best: place primary emphasis on relationships. By pursuing relationships first, they almost always enjoy increased results. And the rewards follow the results.

Think of those organizing principles as a process. The most effective order becomes: relationships, results, and rewards. Through building strong relationships, we not only enjoy the benefits of friendship, but we create for ourselves a network of people and a team of colleagues and vendors who are interested in helping us succeed. Why? Because they like us, perhaps, but because they also know we have their best interests in mind as well.

2. Make meaning out of making money

The 80 year old proprietor, unlit cigar in hand, shuffled towards the back of the restaurant with a slight stoop. He glanced my direction and said, "Let me check on your order." Moments earlier he had narrated a tour of the photos of family, friends and the famous who had dined at his restaurant. The photos, some old and yellow, others crisp and new were taped inside the glass cabinet where the cash register sat. He shared the story of each photo as if he were telling it for the first time. Although age had slowed him down, it had not diminished his apparent enthusiasm for what he did

I had dined there the night before. This restaurant was ordinary in appearance like any other café in any other small town with the exception of the bright and dated neon sign out front. It had been recommended by a client who told me that the place was "a hole in the wall" but that the food was excellent.

My first visit I dined on gumbo, assorted seafood, wonderful fresh-baked rolls and ice box pie. I was the last diner to leave at 9:30 p.m. The 80 year old proprietor, according to his son who was working that night, was the only one still living of the three brothers who had founded the place. While the building it occupied was historic, the neighborhood was rough. "I keep telling my father we need to find a new location, but he'll hear nothing of it," his son had told me with resignation.

I came back for lunch the following day. Business was brisk and the food was, as before, extraordinary. The preparation was simple but the taste was rich. The food and ambiance I experienced made me think of other restaurants, some of the finest seafood restaurants in the world. Suddenly those other restaurants seemed sterile in comparison. The captains of industry could not have been happier and more alive than Mike. In his humble surroundings, he was clearly enjoying himself: telling stories, greeting regulars, admonishing a lazy busboy.

I realized what a rare sight I was observing.

I work with managers, leaders, movers and shakers. I see them in paneled offices or contemporary meetings rooms, cooled to the perfect temperature and attended to by assistants who make sure that every reasonable need is met. They wear well tailored clothes that look good on their health-club-toned bodies. In every way, their surroundings and appearance are superior to the interior of that café—with one notable exception. They all lacked the pure enjoyment of work expressed by the café owner.

Where is the joy of work today? The enjoyment is not inherent in the work; it must be injected into it by our own efforts.

Curiously, I rarely see my clients and colleagues enjoying what they do. I'm not saying they don't enjoy what they do—I just don't see it. Whatever enjoyment there may be isn't apparent. Given their salaries and possessions, they should be getting a kick out of their lives, but appearances are to the contrary.

Where is the joy of work today? While not completely absent, it seems well-hidden. Successful highly paid professionals delay any gratification until they arrive home after a tedious rush hour commute. If they aren't too tired to interact, they enjoy a few brief hours with spouse and kids unless they fall victim to the numbing passivity of TV.

I don't want to belittle the plight of the unemployed, or those who have few choices about the work they do to survive. But I do believe, that for the majority of Americans, including you the reader, it is easier to make money than it is to make meaning. Earning a living today is easier than enjoying it. The enjoyment is not inherent in the work. As with the example of the café owner, it must be injected into it by our own efforts. One of the greatest challenges of modern work life is to find career success and life significance in the same place.

3. Make the most of every moment

"We don't choose to be role models, we are chosen. Our only choice is whether to be a good role model or a bad one."

– Karl Malone

I had just finished speaking on the fifty yard line of the Atlanta Georgia Dome. A group of 100 highly creative "techies" (not an oxymoron) had gathered for a departmental meeting.

After talking with a few audience members, a man near the field entrance approached me. He extended his hand and said, "I'm one of the bus drivers. They didn't really invite us to attend your presentation, but I stood in the back of the room anyway. I like hearing speakers and learning new ideas. I want you to know that you really encouraged me. You see, I'm an inventor. I've invented a new seat cushion people can use when attending events in stadiums just like this one. And I agreed with practically everything you said. Your words have encouraged me to keep trying."

The client was very happy with my presentation that day. But the biggest reward came not from the fee I received, but from the feedback of an appreciative individual who wasn't even supposed to be in the audience.

You just never know who's watching and listening. Our lives are speeches of sorts that we consciously give to a chosen audience. But these living speeches have a subtle power to make significant differences to many outside our intended audience, and often that occurs when we are least cognizant of it.

This reminds me of a profound discovery I had made years ago. Before I became self-employed I held two jobs. One came as a phone call right out of the blue to interview at a company in the east. I got hired. Much later I learned what prompted the president to call me. He said, I was having breakfast at a trade show. Some young guy walked into the restaurant to meet a client. I was so taken with his confidence and style, I figured, that's the kind of person we need here. I checked around to find out who he was and who he worked for. You were that guy." I remember the time and place he was referring to. It was an early breakfast meeting with a less than memorable client. And I couldn't have guessed that that particular moment would be a defining one. But it was and I didn't even know it was happening at the time.

Every moment can be a defining moment if we choose to make them so.

4. Don't pay too much

Is it possible to pay too much to better your best? Yes. There are always some prices that are too high to pay.

If you aren't having fun, you've paid too much. Not every moment invested in bettering your best will be pleasurable, but the process should be fun. If it isn't, you're not doing it right.

You've paid too much if, in the process, you lose your respect for others. High performers have high standards. It is easy to look down on others without the same ambition or commitment, but it's wrong. Be a role model, inspire those you can, but don't try to impose your ambitions on others. Value people for the diversity they bring to the human party. Live respectfully of others.

You've paid too much if your health is diminished. If you're focus becomes maniacal and causes you to eat poorly, exercise seldom and diminish the temple of the body, you are paying too much for improvement and success.

You've paid too much if you lose the love and respect of those people most important to you. Leaving your family and friends on the altar of success would be the saddest and most severe price you could pay.

You've paid too much if you move further away from your Creator. I believe we have the astounding capacity to create by design. Your highest inspiration to create will come when you realize that you are a co-creator with the most powerful force in the universe. As C.K. Chesterton said, "Without God, man can not. Without man, God will not."

Bored or Bold—the Choice Is Yours

"Boredom is a matter of choice, not circumstance."

- Elbert Hubbard

Bruno Gouvy died June 15, 1990 while attempting an extreme snowboard descent in Chamonix, France. His death was tragic, but the words he shared about risk and his philosophy of life live on:

"In western civilization we lead very structured lives. I think laws are good—they hold society together. But I also think that from time to time we need to touch a more primitive instinct. On the cliff face you are your own authority. There is no policeman, judge or lawyer to give you permission. You must decide for yourself.

Many people lead lives of monotony and dullness punctuated by brief periods of excitement and fulfillment.

Sure, there is a chance I might be killed. But in exchange, I have such a powerful sense of being alive. It's a bargain. I look at the risk, I take every step to minimize it, and in exchange for this little risk, I receive such a huge joy in living. Without risk, the sun is just the sun, grass is just grass. With risk, common things have incredible freshness."

Many people lead lives of monotony and dullness punctuated by brief periods of excitement and fulfillment, but don't you and I desire to lead a life of excitement and significance interrupted by the fewest possible moments of monotony? While the risks you and I view as acceptable vary, the point remains the same: It isn't about what happens each day, but rather what you make happen—or make of what happens.

Carpe Diem—Seize the day.

"Death is not the greatest loss in life. The greatest loss is what dies inside us while we live."

– Norman Cousins

Some time ago in Australia I tried bungee jumping and discovered that I really enjoy it. I've also learned from it. On my first, nervous jump, ankles tied and my toes dangling over the edge of a specially-built jumping bridge, I made an important discovery. There are actually two kinds of commitment. The first is intellectual commitment. That's how you feel at the end of the speech or sermon or when you've finished reading an inspirational book. In your head, you're a new person, willing and ready to act. That is, however, not the most important commitment.

There is a second kind of commitment I call pragmatic commitment. This is a commitment based on action, determined by what you do with the information inside your head. Nike's classic ad campaign was right. Pragmatic commitment demands that you quit thinking about it and analyzing it, considering it and contemplating it. Pragmatic commitment says once you've done your homework and set your course, the pivotal time arrives when you must JUST DO IT.

You and I are on the edge every day, and it isn't about bungee jumping. We're on the edge when it comes to dealing with the challenges of life in a changing world. Many of these changes we have little or no control over. We're on the edge in our work. Our employers demand more, as do our customers and colleagues. We're on the edge when it comes to fulfilling our commitments to our families, our churches and our communities. Not least of all, we're on the edge when it comes to living the kind of life of which we are capable; of reaching our true potential, of becoming the best we can be and still finding ways to get better.

There is a difference between being on the edge like this and bungee jumping. In bungee jumping, you can change your mind, chicken out, or call it what you may. They'll keep your money, but they'll let you walk back down the stairs of the bridge.

Our lives aren't like that. We have to shift our focus from the fear of jumping to the pleasures and rewards that follow the leap. Life, symbolic of our responsibilities, commitments, dreams and desires, stands behind us each day, and you feel life's hands on your back. Life whispers in your ear, "You're going to go over again today. You've got no choice about that. But I will give you one choice. It is the choice you've always had and always will have. I'll let you choose how you go."

My final challenge to you, and my fondest hope, is that every time you find yourself on the edge, you'll not struggle or fall, but instead you'll take this advice:

Leap boldly!

George Santayana said, "There is no cure for birth and death save to enjoy the interval." Enjoy the journey.

And may you always strive to be the best at what you do—and still keep getting better. That's the essence of upgrading.

About the Author

Mark Sanborn, CSP, CPAE

Because of his ability to educate and entertain simultaneously, Mark Sanborn is known internationally as *the high-content speaker who motivates.*

Mark is the president of Sanborn & Associates, Inc., an idea lab for leadership development.

He has written 4 books, co-authored 7 books, and is the author of more than 20 videos and numerous audio training programs on leadership, change, teamwork and customer service. His book titles include: *Teambuilt: Making Teamwork Work*, *The Fred Factor: Every Person's Guide to Making the Ordinary Extraordinary*, *Sanborn On Success* and *Meditations for the Road Warrior*. He has presented over 1700 speeches and seminars in every state and 10 foreign countries.

Mark is a regular columnist for *Life @ Work* magazine and a contributing editor of *Sales & Marketing Excellence.*

He is a member of the prestigious Speakers Roundtable, 20 of the top speakers in the world today. Mark holds the Certified Speaking Professional (CSP) from the National Speakers Association and is a member of the exclusive Speaker Hall of Fame (CPAE).

Mark serves on the board of U.S. Learning, a Memphis-based corporate university developer and is a founding professor of MentorU.com, an Internet based learning company. He is a member of the National

Speakers Association Board of Directors and serves as chair of the NSA Center for Professional Development.

His clients include ADP, Cisco, Costco, Enterprise Rent-A-Car, Exxon, Harley-Davidson, Hewlett Packard, Mortons of Chicago, New York Life, ServiceMaster, Washington Mutual and Wells Fargo.

His presentation titles include:

- ★ High Impact Leadership
- ★ The Leadership Experience
- ★ The 10 Commandments of Customer Service
- ★ Making Teamwork Work
- ★ Mastering Change
- ★ The Fred Factor
- ★ and, of course, Upgrade!

He and his wife Darla and sons Hunter and Jackson live in Highlands Ranch, Colorado and are members of Cherry Hills Community Church.

Contact Mark at:
Sanborn & Associates, Inc.
818 E. Summer Drive
Highlands Ranch, CO 80126
303.683.0714
fax 303.683.0825
mark@marksanborn.com

For Upgrade! updates, recent articles and much more, please visit his website at
www.marksanborn.com

LEARNING RESOURCES BY MARK SANBORN

(for a complete list of resources, please visit www.marksanborn.com)

BOOKS

Upgrade! Proven Strategies for Dramatically Increasing Personal and Professional Success $15.95
Teambuilt: Making Teamwork Work $12.95
Meditations for the Road Warrior $14.95
Outlaw Wisdom $9.95
The Outlaws of Success $9.95

AUDIOS

How to Manage Your Time, Energy & Relationships (two tapes) $19.95
Speak Like a Pro (four tapes) $49.95
The 10 Commandments of Customer Service (one tape) $10.95

VIDEOS

Service Leadership (three tapes) $159
High Impact Leadership (three tapes) $249
workbooks .... $5 ea.
Teambuilding: How to Motivate and Manage People (three tapes) $249
workbooks .... $5 ea.
Mastering Change (two videos) $149.95
workbooks .... $5 ea.

Free with any order over $50 — Outlaw Wisdom!

Plus U.S. Shipping & Handling
International Shipping & Handling varies

To order or for more information about Mark's books, tapes, speeches and training sessions contact:

Sanborn & Associates, Inc.
818 E. Summer Drive
Highlands Ranch, CO 80126
(800) 650-3343 • Fax (303) 683-0825
email: MarkSpeaks@aol.com
http://www.marksanborn.com